OFFBEAT IN ASIA

OFFBEAT IN ASIA

An Excursion

MICHAEL ALEXANDER

DAVID McKAY COMPANY, INC.

NEW YORK

DS
49.7
.A7
1960

PRINTED IN GREAT BRITAIN
SET IN 11 POINT GARAMOND
BY EBENEZER BAYLIS & SON LTD., THE TRINITY PRESS,
WORCESTER, AND LONDON

915.0 A12

CONTENTS

ILLUSTRATIONS

All photographs are the copyright of the author

*The German scholar Gregorovius sees the Shah of Persia
in the station at Traunstein.*
'We stood opposite the carriage anxious to obtain
a sight of the successor of Darius and Xerxes.
The Shah himself opened the window and spoke
to us in French; asked about the place, the
country, the King of Bavaria. After each answer,
he turned round to someone whom we could not
see and said, "Notez" . . .'

From his Journal (1873)

To Diana, with love

'A la recherche du temps perdu'

PRELUDE: THE ISTANBUL HILTON

THE BEST hotel in Europe is American, a truncated skyscraper stuck on a landscaped spur in upper Istanbul. Its several terraces and six hundred or so windows give an uninterrupted view of the Bosphorus, five minutes across whose ferry-churned waters the geographical expression called Asia begins its slow unfolding.

The starlit panorama from the twenty-storey-high rooftop bar must rank with man's most spectacular. From that high place 'all the kingdoms of the world and all the glory of them' seem to be laid out below. The broad waters of the Bosphorus are pinpricked with the portholes of cruise liners and Black Sea coasters; fat round mosques and their attendant exclamatory minarets are placed at exactly the right intervals along the skyline; across the water what looks like a Luna Park infers frivolity; a gasometer (like an iron mosque) in the foreground suggests the functional; over to the right a blue neon Air France sign implies the international; and immediately below, floodlit flowerbeds and coloured pools and fountains contribute a Technicolor but not impossibly ostentatious coda to the main composition. Sensational! Cinemascopic! Almost sublime! The view should be saluted with a glass of champagne obtainable at a high price from the crystal-studded bar behind . . .

All this and more inside was heady stuff to two ingenuous travellers just in from the dusty, bumpy road through Yugoslavia and Salonika, an eight-day journey from England that might have been accomplished in six had we not lingered by the blue Aegean. Finally installed at the Hilton we were tempted to surrender body and soul to so comfortable a cathedral of materialism, reserving Byzantium, the Blue Mosque, Santa Sofya, the Covered Bazaar and all the other touristic 'musts' that squatted in the surrounding sub-fusc for our return journey. For the present it seemed there was plenty to investigate on the immediate premises, whose wide range of amenities—*vide* the small booklet that came with the key and a voucher for a free 'Bosphorus Cocktail'—included the following:

MARMARA ROOF

This intimate bar offers one of the most beautiful views in the world—a panoramic picture of Istanbul, the Bosphorus, the Princes Islands, the Sea of Marmara, and the asiatic coast. Open for cocktails before lunch until the small hours of the morning. Dancing after 11 p.m.

SKY GARDEN

During the summer months, among colourful sub-tropical flora, one can relax and sunbathe on lounge chairs and sun couches.

BOSPHORUS TERRACE HOUSE

Located on the main entrance lobby level overlooking the Bosphorus; here cocktails, American Soda Fountain specialities and snacks are served in a pleasantly informal atmosphere which is as casual as the corner drugstore.

LALEZAR TULIP ROOM

This Turkish Lounge, decorated in a style reminiscent of the Old Turkish atmosphere, is situated adjacent to the main lounge and writing room. Ideal for sipping delicious Turkish coffee, playing bridge or just reading.

SADIRVAN SUPPER CLUB

Istanbul's only American-Style Supper Club is located on the Garden Entrance level between the reflection pools. Delectable Turkish, American and International dishes together with excellent music and entertainment in an elegant setting are special attractions for all.

SADIRVAN GARDEN OPEN AIR SUPPER CLUB

This outdoor dining terrace offers a most attractive view of the Bosphorus. A truly intimate and romantic terrace with fine foods, wines and service.

TERRACE RESTAURANT

The main restaurant is located on the Garden Entrance level opposite the Elevator lobby. Menus offer a select Turkish and International cuisine and service with choice wines.

KARAGOZ BAR

Is situated immediately opposite the garden floor lobby elevators. This small and intimate bar offers a wide selection of Turkish and International beverages.

ROOM SERVICE

Service at the Istanbul Hilton is not just an empty word. We endeavour to anticipate your every wish, and make your stay with us all the more enjoyable. Please call Extension 39 and a multi-lingual Order Taker will gladly handle your food and beverage requirements.

SPORTS CLUB

Invigorating freshwater swimming in a magnificent free style mosaic-tiled pool with full cabana and bar service is a special feature of the Club. Tennis, table tennis, shuffleboard, archery, clock-golf, putting and a children's enclosure are a few of the many facilities available. Skating and curling in winter.

SHOPPING SERVICE

A group of smart speciality shops, for your convenience, is located in the Patio. Included are the beauty parlour, barber shop and shoeshine stand, news stand, drugstore, Turkish bazaar (gift shop), men's haberdashery, ladies accessories, florist, travel agent and airline offices, banks, etc.

I selected the Sadirvan Supper Club for our first meal, where an Egyptian lady called Scheherezade was billed to do a *danse-de-ventre*. Overcome by the ten-page menu of 'delectable Turkish, American and International dishes' I ordered caviar at 35 lira (about £2) a spoonful (3.5 lira had seemed a reasonable price considering the Black Sea was a fairly plentiful source of sturgeon). The friendly waiter was amused when I discovered my mistake and sympathetic when I complained that such a price was beyond my pocket. He consoled me by saying:

'I think you are English. You have such gentle voices.' As if to say, I think, that the Americans, who formed ninety per cent of the clientele at the Hilton, did not have gentle voices, and that he would rather a gentle voice than gold. Not all Americans have ungentle voices, but in the Sadirvan Supper Club that night snatches of conversation seemed to bounce from the surrounding tables like brickbats—abrupt, adenoidal and 'on the ball'.

'. . . They [in S. India] live like animals in mud huts . . . don't seem to put any energy into what they do . . . but given purpose and direction . . .'

'. . . why, the Turkish army is so big that even the Top Turk couldn't count it . . . they've got the Bosphorus so sewn up that even a quarter of a Russian couldn't get in . . .'

'. . . the strength of the Party cannot be accurately assessed by the noomerical aggregate of its members . . .'

'. . . Owen Lattimore . . . Chiang-Kai-Shek . . . treason . . .'

'. . . NATO . . . WHO . . . Point 4 . . . Baghdad Pact . . . ICBM . . .'

'. . . Hey! Waiter! Is this chicken fried in engine oil? . . .'

Scheherazade's navel was shaped like a crescent and commanded a respectful silence from the diners. We left early and after a final salute to the view, went to bed.

The Turks had spent their last American loan and had not quite brought off the next (they had successfully achieved this by the time of our return some three months later), consequently the shops were empty of goods involving foreign exchange. Splendid showrooms, built at great expense by export-minded corporations in Britain and America, had nothing to offer but prestige. Even lesser luxuries such as cameras and films were unobtainable, though there were a large number of photographers whose windows were filled with hand-tinted portraits of Turkish beauties, family groups and young men in uniform. While I was unsuccessfully trying to buy a puncture outfit in the Street of a Thousand and One Spare Parts, Diana wandered off to buy postcards, of which there was no deficiency whatever.

I had given her the task of decoying representative specimens of society and she soon picked up (or rather was picked-up by) her first victim, a young American called Brewster (his Christian name, I think). He had used the 'it-isn't-safe-to-be-walking-around-here-on-your-own' approach, pointing out that but for his escort some devilish Turk would stick a syringe into her and carry her off to his harem.

'You're a bit on the thin side for Turkish tastes,' he had continued, 'so they'd fatten you up on boiled chestnuts for a few weeks or else pack you off to a brothel on the Gold Coast!'

He had gone on to explain how that was what had happened to the prettiest of the refugees from the Hungarian revolution almost as soon as they set foot in Istanbul. Diana, who had noticed a tendency among Turkish manhood to stare at her acquisitively and at the same time contrive to bump into her, gladly accepted his protection from the threatened *piqûre* and finally, like a good retriever, brought him back to our rendezvous by the swimming pool.

Although the May sun was hot by any standard the enormous pool, shaped like a wet footprint, was forbidden to swimmers 'by order of the management' because the already crystal-clear water had to be changed and chlorinated. Meanwhile the local youth and beauty lounged around in what was termed the 'Sports Area', taking playfully surreptitious plunges into the intarsia-tiled depths whenever the 'Sports Manager' was looking the other way. One side of the pool was lined with a bar, the other with *cabanas*—super-cabins each equipped with bathroom and bedroom and fronted by a private piece of terrace patterned with comfortable chairs and divided from its neighbour by a trellis of morning glory. Number One in the row was permanently leased to an American airline for the inter-flight relaxation of its aircrews and trim little air hostesses with neat black shoes, bobbed hair and tiny travelling bags would come in after some long flight and emerge as Aquabelles to lie around in the sun. Brewster, who seemed to have a wide acquaintance among them, edged us in that direction.

'But you should see the Greek Line girls!' he enthused, when I expressed interest. 'They know how to take care of themselves. You know, not too much make-up! Marvellous legs the Greek girls have!'

A blonde called Sandra had just got in from New York and we lay around at her feet. We were immediately joined by Ergun, the local Turkish Lothario, who also had had an eye for legs and soon made an encircling movement around Diana's. I asked if it were true what Brewster had said about all the Hungarian girls being kidnapped for the bordellos. Ergun, who spoke quite good American, said:

'It burns me up to hear that story going around! There *was* something in the papers about a couple of girls disappearing. But it turned out they were working in a cabaret where they had taken a job voluntarily. Brewster tells that tale to everybody. I shouldn't wonder if he didn't run a brothel some place himself.'

Despite this ardent defence of Turkish rectitude Ergun turned out to be a Turk with a sense of humour. They are a dour, uncompromising race on the whole, like a cross between the Scots

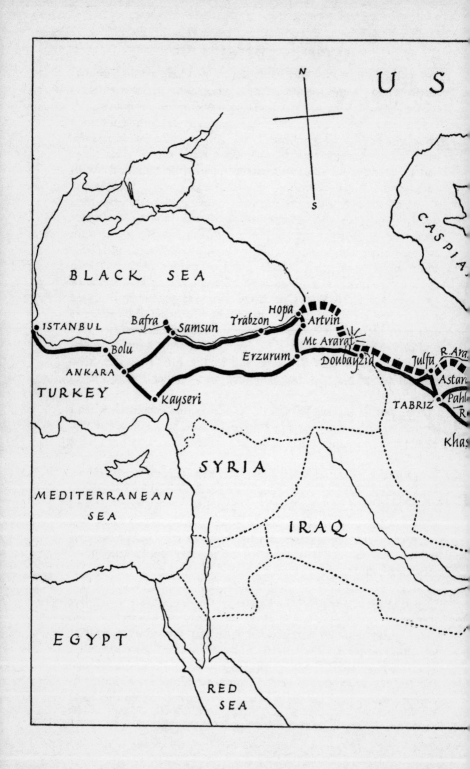

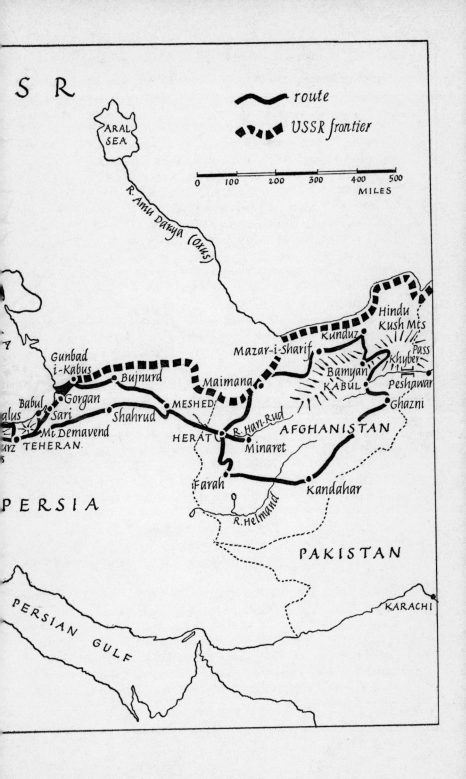

and the Swedes. They lack finesse. Generally speaking, especially in the Middle East, it is not too difficult, if you have any ability to mime, to carry on quite advanced conversations without a common language. The Turks have many qualities, but self-expression is not among them: ask a Turk a question and the chances are he will throw his head back with a rat-trap jerk and say 'yok', then he will pause a moment while he readies his epiglottis for a second jab and a second 'yok'. All of which looks and sounds like a reluctant 'yes', but is in fact a categoric 'no'. 'Evet', the more rarely used affirmative, is habitually delivered with a hiss and is accompanied by a negative shake of the head.

Ergun, who was safe to tease about such things, did his best to adjust the balance with what was perhaps an excess of American heartiness. After buying us all drinks and paying a profusion of continental-style compliments to the girls, he bounced off in his white shorts for a game of tennis with the 'Professor', tennis champion of Turkey for seven years running and in his retirement coach at the Hilton. Tennis was Ergun's great game; he begged us to send him some balls from England—best in the world, he said, and utterly unobtainable in Turkey.

I was keen to know exactly what Brewster and his brother-Americans, of whom there were a number staying at the Hilton, were doing in Turkey, but I hesitated to ask him too many direct questions as I detected a certain caginess in his replies. From his statement that he wanted to be a teacher and thus 'be of greater service to mankind than flying jets' I deduced the obvious; from general conversation I gathered that he had recently been to Beyrouth 'clocking up flying time' and that there were certain parts of Turkey over which US airmen were forbidden to fly. But from his friend, a talkative Brooklyner of Neapolitan extraction, I learned that the American officers in Turkey were 'very specially selected' and that apart from their job of flying planes they had other duties such as reporting on the attitude of their Turkish hosts. The Neapolitan was anxious to make his work sound as important and exciting as possible and there were references to previous training in atomic science and to the high-flying potential of the planes he flew. Putting together the various pieces of information he imparted I guessed that it was his function to fly into the stratosphere after Russian H-bomb tests and take samples of radioactivity.

Brewster was based on an airfield some way from Istanbul, but he managed nevertheless to put in most of his time at the Hilton, where he had lived for over a year. ('I get eight hundred dollars a month, so I can afford it,' he said, 'and that's more than the average Turkish general can say!') But just now he was worried:

'The management are trying to move me on. I get all my liquor from the PX so they don't make as much out of me as they'd like to. They want my room for the tourists. But,' Brewster warned, 'they'd better not try anything or they'll be hearing from Conrad Hilton. And Conrad is a very great personal friend of a very great personal friend of mine!'

Brewster was a great patron of 'Room Service' and was forever picking up the telephone to ask for ice, or a chicken sandwich, a special record to be played over the relay, or news about the arrival of the next Pan-Am plane. The staff seemed to jump rapidly to his requests with the exception of the 'housekeeper', a stern Swiss lady looking like Paula Wessely, who he suspected had ganged up with the manager.

'Room service is falling off!' was one of Brewster's frequent remarks, 'God knows what will happen when the Turks take this place over!'

This reference to the Turks 'taking the place over' is best expanded by the little book already quoted, which I do not paraphrase for fear of spoiling the subtleties of its phraseology:

A BRIEF HISTORY OF THE ISTANBUL HILTON

The 300-room Istanbul Hilton is the result of close co-operation between the Government of Turkey and American enterprise. The project was undertaken by the Turkish Government and assigned to the nation's Pension Fund for administration. The original agreement was signed in Ankara, Turkey, on December 15 1950 by Feyzi Lutfi Karamanoglu, Turkish Minister of State and John W. Houser, executive vice-president of Hilton Hotels International Inc. Ground-breaking ceremonies were held on April 16 1951 and the Hotel was officially opened to the public on June 10 1955.

The entire cost of the completed Hotel, including all furniture, equipment, and installations, was borne by the owners, the Turkish Republic Pension Fund, to a total of

approximately 7,000,000 dollars, and the beautiful site for
the Hotel was made available by the Turkish Grand National
Assembly. The Hilton organization is operating the Hotel
on the basis of a twenty-year lease.

From the Hotel's inception to the official opening, the
Hilton organization planned the design and engineering with
the American architectural firm of Skidmore, Owings, and
Merrill and their Turkish associate, Sedad H. Eldem, award-
winning contemporary architect. Hilton Hotels International
also supplied the working capital and inventories of supplies,
food and beverages and was responsible for publicizing and
promoting the Hotel. All the experience of the Hilton
organization was incorporated into the planning so that
the Istanbul Hilton would be the most modern hotel in
Europe.

A special design office was set up in the Hotel and the
combined talents of Turkish, American and western European designers produced the blending of Turkish motifs and
modern design in the interiors and furnishings.

A substantial part of all the upholstered furniture was
supplied by the Teachers' Technical College in Ankara and
the 15,000 square yards of carpeting throughout the Hotel
were hand-woven in Konya, one of the centres of Turkey's
carpet industry. Most of the other equipment and furnishings, including textiles and lamps, were imported from many
European countries and from the United States.

Prior to the opening of the Hotel, Hilton Hotels International organized an intensive training program jointly
sponsored by the Pension Fund, the ECA and the Hilton
organization. Some twenty young Turkish men and women
spent over a year in various departments of Hilton Hotels in
the United States, training for such key positions as Assistant
Manager, Front Office Manager, Personnel Manager, Purchasing Director, Telephone Supervisor, Housekeeper,
General Accounting and Analysis Manager, and Night
Manager. They, in turn, trained their staff upon returning to
Turkey. Following the Hilton custom of recruiting staff from
the people of the country in which a hotel is located, practically all of the Istanbul Hilton employees are Turkish.

In addition to being a focal point for business, diplomatic, tourist functions, the Istanbul Hilton Hotel is a living symbol of close friendship between Turkish and American people.

'Close friendship between Turkish and American people', apparently one of the purposes behind the hotel's construction, became most tangible around tea-time when the 'Turkish Lounge' and the 'Bosphorus Terrace' became the scene of a thrice-weekly *thé dansant*. This function was heavily patronized by the citizens of Istanbul, who would crowd the little tables, drink tea, chat and eat complicated cakes. There was a band, but I cannot recall having seen anybody dance. The customers were smartly dressed but stuffy, and the atmosphere was somehow reminiscent of Berne at its most bourgeois. The more *mondaine* members of local society appeared at cocktail time or after dinner in the rooftop room.

'You can find women alone up there,' Brewster said enthusiastically. 'You might easily get picked up by a Princess.'

Otherwise the impeccably decorated lobbies were thronged with to'ing-and-fro'ing Americans: Gregory Pecks from NATO with well-cut uniforms and chins, hawk-eyed men with missions and brief-cases, thin-lipped Daughters of the Revolution irrepressibly interested in just everything and everybody, groups of tourists off a cruise liner from Tel Aviv, sailors in immaculate white ducks from visiting U.S. warships (there was no discrimination against enlisted men at the Hilton), and a lot of apparently unattached children—nasty little boys with crewcuts and pert little girls trying to look sexy several years ahead of schedule. The English rarely infiltrated this citadel of the American Way of Life —('Eengleesh can't afford! Who else but Americans would stay at a dump like this?'—the smartly-dressed Turkish doorman who had worked in Columbus, Ohio, said disparagingly when I questioned him on my immediate arrival). The Island Race lurked in the older hotels down the road like the Park and the Pera Palas. In fact, the only Englishman I met at the Hilton was a young Jew (he wore a gold Star of David round his neck) called Mark, who represented a firm of Leeds tailors and was officially accredited to the American forces in Turkey to supply them with English-made suits. He wandered round their messes with a book of samples and a very friendly manner and claimed to be doing several thousand dollars' worth of business a week. He couldn't wait to get back to an English pub. . . .

2

ANKARA

ASIA beckoned beyond the Bosphorus. The breezy upper deck of the streamlined car-ferry overlooked a champagne-sparkling seascape, unconfined by the opposing continental coastlines. To the east, beyond the old lighthouse, the Sea of Marmara opened up to let in the fresh breezes of the Mediterranean; westwards the strategic waterway, subject of so many superannuated treaties regarding the rights of passage of the Powers, cut through to the Russian-bordered Black Sea. Opposite was the mosque-studded suburb of Uskudar, Florence Nightingale's Scutari. Here the ferryboat back-pedalled into its berth, let down its flat nose, and we clattered off expectantly into Asia Minor.

Embassy officials and others with fast cars make the journey to Ankara, three hundred miles eastwards on the Anatolian plateau, in seven hours. The road is tarred though not always in good condition (there is no word for 'maintenance' in the Turkish language); it is hoped that when Wimpey, the British construction company, whose yellow machines studded the route like giant antediluvian insects, have finished the job urgent officials will be able to cut their journey by an hour. But we had made a late start and our limited speed made the capital impossible to attain that day. We had heard of an interesting hotel at Abant, high in the hills above Bolu, and decided to sleep there. It was on a lake and the Turkish tourist map marked it with a little pine tree, which did not necessarily denote the presence of a pine tree, though in fact there were many, but was a symbol for a place of 'scenic interest'. It was already dusk when we turned off the main road and up into the wooded hills. There was little more than a track, but excavations and slumbering bulldozers indicated that the construction of a more serious road was in hand. We climbed up among the conifers for about an hour, until the lights of the lonely hotel came into sight.

The Abant hotel was said to be popular at summer week-ends when the citizens of Ankara escape to the hills from the heat. It was built entirely of wood and the inside was like a packing-case, the walls made of compressed wood shavings. We had dinner in the large wooden dining-room, empty but for the almost tangible presence of Atatürk pictured in brown riding clothes beside a big brown horse. The image of the founder of modern Turkey, who died in 1938, still watches over his people from innumerable Turkish walls. Usually the 'Father of the Turks' looks out, rugged and perhaps a little crafty, from above a stiff shirt and tailcoat. Atatürk Militant is comparatively rare.

Two or three Turks were sitting in the lounge listening to jazz on the wireless. They seemed to be enjoying it, but when a Beethoven concert began they hurriedly tuned in to whining Turkish music that came discordantly to my ear even after practice. Atatürk, in his efforts to westernize Turkey, once forbade the playing of Oriental music just as he did the wearing of the veil and the *tarbush*. He allowed it to be reintroduced, so the story goes, following the unofficial visit to Istanbul of the Duke of Windsor and Mrs Simpson in 1936. The Duke—next to Winston Churchill and Princess Margaret, England's most popular personality in Turkey—told the Dictator how sorry he was that he never heard any Turkish music. Such lofty endorsement caused Atatürk to encourage again those mournful cadences, which, in Turkey, where few of the visual trappings of the Orient remain, seem sadly displaced.

The following morning, after a breakfast of omelette, cheese and cherry jam, we walked down to the lake. Grassy banks backed by pine woods gave it an Austrian ambiance and the crisp, sunny air was as invigorating as an Alpine spring. We decided to make the three-mile circuit of the lake and investigate what the brochure described as 'the abundant wild-life'. It must have been the wrong time of year, for apart from some duck flushed by Diana walking barefoot through the oily reeds and some white birds by the waterside, which I suspect were egrets, there was nothing of interest, unless one included the *agapemones* of frogs which clustered in the hot shallows, mounting their loves with passionate and poignant 'YOKS', only momentarily silenced when the purposeful swoop of a hooded crow depleted their number by one.

We swam from the landing stage below the hotel, and did not continue our journey until after lunch.

Soon after our departure we were stopped by a band of foresters with ragged clothes and fierce Montenegrin moustaches, supporting a groaning comrade. His leg had been crushed beneath a falling tree and a blood-soaked puttee bore witness to his distress. We were asked to take him to the construction camp below, so Diana sat on the bonnet while the invalid got in beside me. Then we wound slowly down to the camp, where there was a lorry to take him to the doctor in Bolu.

Reaching the main road I discovered that a small case, carelessly thrown into the back to make room for the damaged man, had come open and all its contents had fallen out on the way. We were forced to retrace our route, stopping every few hundred yards to pick up a lipstick, a toothbrush, a looking-glass, which had miraculously escaped the wheels of the many bullock carts creaking down the road with giant pine logs in tow, and the acquisitive eyes of their drivers. We recovered in this way all the objects with the exception of a small purse containing about six pounds in Turkish money. I had resigned myself to its loss when, on the way down again, we were stopped at the camp and there it was—picked up by a passing carter and handed in to the foreman. Thereafter if ever Turkish national honesty was in question we ardently defended it with this simple illustration.

Ankara, planted by Atatürk on a bare plain ringed by treeless hills, was attained in darkness. We drove through the illuminated trappings of metropolis, up the great central boulevard lined with large modern buildings, past the modern Opera House, to the first hotel we could find, a barrack-like building called the Ararat Oteli. Its amenities were indicated when an American soldier knocked at the door and asked Diana if she was 'Maria', as he had an appointment with a lady of that name.

Next morning I paid a call on the British Embassy, known locally as the Sefaret-i-Britannia, at the top of a hill completely covered in Embassies, to find out my chances of being allowed by the Turkish authorities to travel to Iran via the Black Sea and the Russian frontier zone. This was not the normal route, but I was committed to attempt it as my publisher, who, after all, was paying for the trip, had directed me to follow as closely as possible what he called 'The Underbelly of the Bear', that is the frontiers of Turkey, Iran, and Afghanistan contiguous to Soviet Russia. Atatürk, building a nation to include such dissident elements as Armenians and Kurds, discouraged visitors from travelling east of Ankara. But with the coming to power of the Democratic

Party in 1950 restrictions on movement had been largely lifted and
there seemed a fair chance of my being allowed to visit other than
the most exclusively military areas. I particularly wanted to go
through Kars, the rocky fortress that in the last four wars with
Russia had taken the brunt of the opening moves in the cam-
paigns.

The Embassy, busy with the Cyprus Question and the rehearsal
of an Ian Hay play, implied that official permission might take a
long time in coming and unless I was prepared to spend a week
or more lobbying government officials, I should be advised to set
off and hope for the best. The concrete cauldron of Ankara, with
little to offer the tourist other than a wide choice of Banks
(ranging architecturally from neo-Islamic to Bauhaus), an enormous mausoleum dedicated to Atatürk, a park with a parachute
tower and a boating lake shaped like the Bosphorus, and a
museum full of hideous Hittite remains, gave no good reason to
resist this tacit advice. But needing certain information I did not
think there was much to lose by visiting the Press and Tourist
Ministry, which lay at the end of a street known to Embassy folk
as 'The Tail of the Horse', since the back end of a great equestrian
statue of Atatürk directly pointed down it.

I found the Ministry, and kind officials passed me from one
office to another until I found the right person, a plump, hand-
rubbing Ottoman, who talked with an American accent. His
library contained a number of American books as well as Djilas's
The Ruling Class. Above the bookcase was a confusing abstract
painting in blue. Above his desk was Atatürk the Diner-Out.

We had a short talk about the Turkish tourist trade which I
gathered was showing encouraging possibilities. 34,283 Americans
had visited the country in 1956, as against 10,572 British, 10,707
French, 10,635 West Germans, 329 Jordanians, 2,671 Lebanese,
905 Syrians, and 372 Egyptians. After earnestly taking down all
these figures on my knee and refraining to ask if they were not
mainly short-stay visitors from Cruise liners, I came to the question
of travelling to Persia via Kars. This produced much hand rubbing
and a stall, not a categorical YOK but the suggestion that I call
again in the afternoon, following his inquiries. This I did, having
made full allowance for the siesta period, but though I waited
over an hour he did not come.

That evening there was to be a lecture, sponsored by the British

Council, by Britain's major minor poet John Betjeman. I was sorry
to have missed Margot Fonteyn who had reputedly given a
ravishing performance at the Opera House a few days before.
The lecture was to be given in the Faculty of Literature, a modern
building of brown concrete on the Atatürk Boulevard, which
from its massive proportions looked competent to cover the most
recherché literatures of the world. A crowd was collecting near
the main door, where a blue-suited young man bowed us into a
long room filled with elegant chattering people. But instead of a
lecturer to listen to, there were photographs to look at: dynamic
shots of Budapest in blossom time and filtered vistas of the
Hortobagy with forward-looking farmers backed by poplars
bending in the breeze. It soon became clear that this was a rival
entertainment organized by the Hungarians, and though they
made us welcome we felt in duty bound to look for Mr Betjeman.

A label hanging round the neck of a bust of Atatürk announced
that the lecture was taking place on the third floor, so we climbed
the wide flight of marble and followed sporadic arrows that
petered out among baleful statues of Hittite kings. By trial and
error at various doors we came upon a large classroom, where the
lesson we sought was in progress. The room was enormous, high
as a cathedral, and by no means filled, so that the voice of Mr
Betjeman developed a resonance that was impressive but difficult
to understand. Extraneous activities made concentration impossible. A photographer was trying to record the affair with a
loud-whirring 16mm camera, which was proving difficult because the floodlight, operated by a colleague, would give no
more than an occasional blinding flash. Then there were the trains.
More trains than I should have thought ran in the whole of
Turkey shunted back and forth outside the window. As they
passed they hooted mournfully, with a pathos most appropriately
Tennysonian.

Entirely unperturbed, the lecturer, bland as any bishop, boomed
on. The evening sun, sinking behind the Anatolian highlands,
reflected from a balding head; a glint of white tooth pricked
through a mobile mouth; an archiepiscopal finger was raised and
the hall hushed as he mounted the crescendo passage of his
celebrated 'Subaltern's Love Song':

Miss J. Hunter Dunn, Miss J. Hunter Dunn,
Furnish'd and burnish'd by Aldershot sun,
What strenuous singles we played after tea,
We in the tournament—you against me!

Love-30, love-40, oh! weakness and joy,
The speed of a swallow, the grace of a boy,
With carefullest carelessness, gaily you won,
I am weak from your loveliness, Joan Hunter Dunn.

This was rare wine indeed. But would it travel? Would it stand
up to the arid intellectual atmosphere of Ankara? I looked around
me to see if the audience were appropriately moved. The Embassy
English, who formed the large majority, smiled knowing esoteric
smiles, as though members of a cultural conspiracy. The Turks,
identifiable by their non-smiles, seemed to have a suspicion of
victimization. Two pretty schoolgirls at the next desk giggled and
blushed.

Then Mr Betjeman embarked on a set of verses about his
favourite Surrey, whose genteel mysteries he tried to explain by
little pictures on the blackboard—the suburban firs, the gabled
houses, the Rover car. When it was all over and the polite clapping
had ceased we were introduced to the lecturer by Sir John Rothenstein, whose turn it would be to talk the following night.

'What on earth are you doing here?' said Mr Betjeman. He was
gratified to learn that we had travelled from England especially
to hear him lecture.

On the way out I asked the two Turkish girls if they had understood what it was all about. They were students of English
Literature at the Faculty but not, it seemed, at such an advanced
level: they admitted to not having understood a word. But they
thought Mr Betjeman had a nice kind face.

Sir John Rothenstein's lecture, the next evening, was delivered
under even more disadvantageous conditions than Mr Betjeman's.
Not only did the acoustics and a chill caught in the aeroplane
render his voice completely inaudible, but the projected slides
were almost totally invisible. This did not matter so much as the
theme was abstract art, for which, according to Sir John, the
Turks are said to have a predilection (*vide* also my friend at the
Tourist Ministry), though for all anybody in the audience could

tell, the lecturer might have been talking about fretwork. He was booked to repeat his talk in Jerusalem, where I hope he was better served.

After the lecture we had dinner with Patrick O'Regan, Press Secretary at the Embassy. In the party were the Polish Ambassador and his wife, an Embassy couple from Beirut who had chosen to spend their leave travelling to Turkey by bus, and Sir John. O'Regan, who looked like a smaller, spryer version of Lord Hailsham, played a most amiable host. After dinner there was music on the HI-FI, first a set of early French madrigals and then some sparkling Scarlatti. At nine o'clock we listened to the news from London—General de Gaulle had just come in with the military coup in Algeria . . . Sputnik 3 was off with a whoosh— The Polish Ambassador and his lady looked a little smug; the English looked embarrassed. A fruity rendering by Kathleen Ferrier of an aria from *The Messiah*, put on, I think, to show that Britain had at least produced a singer, brought me to a more chauvinistic state of mind.

Next morning, before setting off for the Black Sea, I decided to have one more go at the 'Tail of the Horse' which I had now unsuccessfully visited four times. After ten minutes the great man arrived. He seemed to have a busy day ahead of him for after a nod to me he sat down at his desk and gave careful scrutiny to a document that lay before him. Having studied it intently for several minutes, he looked up and said that he had made inquiries and that he could not authorize me to visit Kars since it lay in a military zone, a fact I already knew. As he spoke I could not help reading (albeit upside down) the letter to which he had been giving such earnest attention: 'My dear Argentines— all of you,' it said in curious English, 'I am girl from Japanese and wish so much to see your so wonderful country and I write for informations to help me realize my dreamy plans . . .'

3

SAMSUN

TURKISH buses and lorries, like New Orleans streetcars, have names. We followed a bus named 'Arslan' ('Lion'), whose habitual route was marked in fairground lettering ISTANBUL–SAMSUN. It soon outpaced us and we were left alone among the green hills and fields of growing wheat; it now seemed for the first time that we had shaken off the shackles of European tourism and were launched into the spacious stamping grounds of the professional traveller. Unfamiliar birds appeared, sitting like crotchets along the telegraph wires; especially common was a blue jay-like bird, a species of roller; but our favourites were the little long billed bee-eaters, which I never saw eat a bee, but often watched pouncing down from their perch on the wires to come up with a fat grasshopper. Storks, called *leylaks* by the Turks, constructed their ramshackle nests on rooftops, on minarets and even on telegraph poles. Their ubiquity and general air of seediness detracted from the mystery and remoteness I had always felt these fairy-tale birds possessed.

Diana, who had never travelled further than Paris for the fashion shows, developed an almost lyrical enthusiasm for the country's flora and fauna, so that when we came upon a tortoise crawling across the road she captured it with all the excitement of an Attenborough coming upon a rare armadillo. She kept her prize in a cardboard box but a Turkish boy urgently insisted she release the dangerous beast, showing us the warts on his hands and claiming they were caused by tortoise urine. Though it was a perfectly ordinary tortoise she was sufficiently discouraged to set it loose. We were less successful in our efforts to capture one of the miniature marmot-like creatures that seemed to thrive in all the most inhospitable spots from Turkey to Afghanistan. They had bushy tails and bow legs and would sit up and grin provocatively before hopping off to their holes in the sand. It is said that if you catch one—we were never quick enough—they become tame almost immediately.

How delectable, we thought, to sleep by the Delice River!

We were quickly disillusioned; it proved to be dried-up, smelly and mosquito-haunted. In the end we settled for a field, lured by a heavenly scent, sweet and soporific like pea or beans, but which could not be identified in the darkness which had now descended. Very early in the morning I was woken by hot breath on my face and a heavy panting in my ear. Shyly opening an eye I saw what looked like an enormous polar bear. I did not move, pretending to be dead. It was in fact an Anatolian sheepdog, white and shaggy, big as a St Bernard; a breed much prized by their owners who reputedly will not part with them at any price. They are fierce, wild dogs who will have no truck with the unfamiliar, and they had on several occasions hurled themselves at the car with apparent intent to kill. American personnel were issued with revolvers for their protection, with orders to shoot if necessary. This one had a guilty conscience; it nosed shiftily under my make-shift pillow and furtively extracted a piece of bread.

The sun came up and birds started singing in many unfamiliar voices; sheepbells tinkled as the shepherd (it was his dog) started his day. All around us were revealed the source of the smell that had drawn us there—night-scented stocks growing like weeds among the grasses.

Over the hills and far away, through nut country down into tobacco country, we came to Samsun, and dropped down a hill flanked with army encampments with sweating soldiers charging suspended sacks with the bayonet. Below was the Black Sea. Directly across those blue waters Soviet citizens were sunning themselves on the beach at Sochi.

A Turkish destroyer, *Mʃo8*, lay anchored off the town, and we watched the big steamer from Istanbul steaming out on its port-hopping journey along the coast. Down among the red-tiled roofs we found a pleasant enough hotel called the Moderne.

The first person we met at the hotel was a Scotsman called Jock. He was laden with cans of beer and tins of fruit on the way to the birthday party of 'one of the boys'. In the short time I was able to talk to him I gathered that he was working on a 'construction job'. This may have been the harbour extensions, for the Americans had decreed that Samsun should be the principal Black Sea port and I had seen cranes and enormous square blocks of concrete on the quay. He was more likely, however, to have been busy on the rocket sites reputedly being constructed along this stretch of coast. He had gone before I could inquire and we were not invited to the party.

Samsun did not beguile. The sea-front was no more than the town's backyard, with a railway track running beside the cindery strand. A market was in progress there, and we could not fail to notice the shoddy quality of the goods and the unattractiveness of the food—revolting by-products of milk, salted fish and wilting vegetables. On a fish stall I prodded a *khalkan*, or 'button-fish', which is only found in the Black Sea. It looked like a turbot covered in carbuncles. According to Lord Curzon it is 'well worth the attention of the most experienced gastronome', so I ordered it in a restaurant, but was told it was out of season.

I had often wondered where all the old clothes went. They go to Turkey and points east, making fine men look like tramps. Many stalls sold terrible cast-off Western suits, browns, pin-stripes and clerical greys, patched, worn and greasy, prime cause of that sleazy decrepitude that characterized the appearance of the Turkish working-man. From flat black cap to rubber galoshes with laces stamped on them to make them look like shoes (worn with the heels down in memory of the slippers they formerly wore), the Turkish worker does not have style. The Anatolian peasants in their traditional brightly-coloured clothes coming in from the country with their produce, no doubt scoffed at by the city slickers, were infinitely more intriguing to the eye.

But Samsun was not without its municipal aspirations. There was a large statue of Atatürk (militant) on a horse; there was a stadium, whither young men and girls carrying banners were marching to fifes and drums in rehearsal of Independence Day celebrations; there was a public garden with palm trees and a zoo consisting of a large cage containing two peacocks and a rabbit; on the beach a hand-operated Ferris wheel made from packing-cases turned forlornly; and on the outskirts a *futbol maçi* was in progress, with virile Turks in bright shirts putting their all into their favourite sport, introduced by British POWs in the 1914–18 war.

Samsun, according to the encyclopedia, was an important centre of the Black Sea caviar industry. I like caviar and I have always felt an interest in the mystic fish whence it is extracted; I had even, in the hope of being able to observe them in their watery haunts, brought with me an underwater mask and schnorkel. Little information on the habits of the sturgeon was available in London, even in the ichthyological library at the Natural History Museum, but I did learn that the Black Sea was second to the Caspian as a major source, and that the Turkish sturgeon spawned in 'early summer' in the rivers Kizilirmak and Yesilirmak. Samsun lay between these two rivers and was named as the chief exporter, but all mention of caviar, which is in fact a Turkish word (*khaviar*), around the town drew only discouraging YOKS.

It might be assumed that fishing took place near the rivers. There was a place called Bafra, about thirty miles to the west on the Kizilirmak, or Red River. I thought I would start my sturgeon safari there.

Bafra was a tobacco town, prosperous and pretty, with red roofs and rambling villas of rich merchants. Our arrival, as was usual when we were in need of official assistance, coincided with *Jummah*, the Moslem day of rest, which falls on a Friday. The narrow streets were full of citizens in their best clothes returning from one of the five regulation daily services. Casting around for clues we were soon surrounded by a milling crowd, who seemed to make no sense of my efforts to explain what I wanted— C-A-V-I-A-R—illustrated by a passable drawing of a sturgeon in the dust. Unsympathetic faces. Uncomprehending grimaces. YOK! YOK!

Then, as always seemed to happen, somebody who made sense turned up—specially summoned perhaps for his experience in dealing with unbelieving, inarticulate, impolite foreigners—and took our problem in hand. Such assistance was usually provided by schoolmasters, but this man, who spoke some English, was a tobacco merchant. I gathered in the course of a difficult conversation that most of his tobacco was exported to Iron Curtain countries whence half of it was re-exported to America to be blended with their native tobacco.

'Why does America not buy direct from us any more?' he asked. I could only guess that it had something to do with currency deficiencies and international trade agreements.

Some pretty little children were playing in a side alley, barefooted and wearing gaudy rags and bangles that might have come straight out of a dressing-up box. Diana, who wasted most of her films photographing children, tried to take a picture of them.

Diana, Istanbul

America in Istanbul: the Hilton Hotel

The Hilton swimming pool bar: M.A. talking to US sailors

Crossing the Bosphorus

But a surly Turk interposed himself between her and them and angrily shooed them away. I protested to our tobacco merchant, but he merely shrugged his shoulders. They were the children of Kurdish gipsies who worked in the tobacco factories and lived in tents outside the town, he said. Only the women worked, and they were quicker and more conscientious than anyone else, but were regarded with suspicion and dislike by the locals.

To start the quest for caviar we were taken to the fish market, opened specially for us, but there was not even a sardine to be seen that day, and all that could be produced was a single rusty tin of the stuff, green and very high, thrust into our faces by a fine old fishmonger in a trilby hat. It was explained, and we gladly accepted the explanation, that this was a reject, not the usual quality, and had been produced simply to interest us. As for the sturgeon, they were brought in the early morning from the fishing village on the estuary, for Bafra was not a port, being four miles from the sea. After several cups of tea in the fishmongers' teahouse our tobacconist was in a mood to take us there.

In company also with a schoolmaster, who wanted to leave something at his school on the way, we drove to the Kizilirmak (which contained not the slightest suggestion of redness) and followed a muddy track along its bank towards the sea. A little higher up, said the tobacco merchant, a small boy had found an enormous fish threshing in the shallows. He had seized the monster round the middle and after a long struggle succeeded in dragging it to the shore. It was a sixty-pound sturgeon and it had already begun to spawn. Twenty pounds of caviar were still inside it, and the boy rushed off to tell his father. The father praised Allah and sold the fish to a passer-by for 200 lira. At Bafra the purchaser passed it on for 1,200 lira. This was a short story, but somehow it took a very long time to tell.

The schoolmaster showed us his school, a little whitewashed building that served the children of the small farmers dotted about the plain. Education is compulsory in Turkey and most of the villages have schools. But at important seasons the children are allowed off lessons to help on the farm. An old iron stove and little wooden desks gave the classroom the atmosphere of a Victorian Dame's school. There were coloured posters on the wall and a map of Turkey's minerals drawn on the board, relic of yesterday's lesson.

We drove on again down a brambly cart-track until the widening river mouth appeared through a reedy marge. A gimcrack
construction of sticks, cane and boards stretched across the estuary
from shore to shore. I took this to be the sturgeon nets, but it
was only a crude barrier to stop the fish getting up the river.
I was soon to see the deadlier hazards that beset them before they
got there.

On the far side a rough boat was pushed into the water and in
response to our signals it came over and took us aboard. A
stalwart fisherman, standing upright at the oars, pulled us over
and we landed on a sandy spit with an oily sea beyond. The air
was heavy and transparent, a retriever-like dog sat mournfully on
the strand, another dog scuffled at the water's edge. I had a
strange feeling I had seen it all before and when a pelican flopped
down in the turgid sea the picture clicked into perspective. It was
the background, almost detail for detail, of Piero da Cosimo's
so-called 'Death of Procris' in the London National Gallery.

We trailed across the sand to the fishing encampment in the
dunes, rude huts of matchwood roofed with branches and reeds.
Led by a sturdy figure with a cap athwart his head, the entire
establishment advanced to meet us. Man and boy they were a
ragged lot, dressed in the worst possible Samsun style. Perhaps
because there were no women among them buttons hung by
threads and bony knees showed through flapping rents. They
had looked fierce at first but when our presence was explained
they became more sociable and the man with the cap, who from
his air of authority I took to be the boss, shook hands and set
himself with gravitas to answer my questions concerning his
trade.

These men, I gathered, were only there for the fishing season:
when there were no sturgeon they farmed or fished the great lake
further up the coast. They were descendants of a tribe of Khazaks,
who left Russia in the days of Catherine the Great, and it seemed
that the jargon of their craft contained many Russian words.
They caught three types of sturgeon, called *mersin*, *sip*, and *sivricka*,
using the hook as their main weapon—a horny hand held up
one of these large and horribly sharp barbs for inspection and
made me feel its point with my finger. These were body hooks,
set at various angles by cork floats; long lines of them are lain
at different depths up to half a mile out to sea across the river

mouth. The unfortunate fish, nosing in towards their spawning grounds, have first to negotiate these wicked hazards. Like submarines in a minefield they may get past some of them but they soon find themselves surrounded and it is only the cunning ones who do not end with a hook through their body. The fish, apparently, do not lose their heads and will laboriously and intelligently edge forwards as though they were solving a puzzle. Should they finally succeed, and on this particular river there were 65,000 hooks to stop them, they come up against the wooden barrier. But in spite of all this, probably as a result of overfishing, it was rare to catch more than six a day. Hence the high price of caviar at the Hilton.

This short course on sturgeon fishing was followed by an alfresco lunch set out on a trestle table under a canopy of branches. The noonday sunlight filtered through the leaves, dappling the shaven heads of the senior fishermen who sat with us. We ate yoghourt thick with chopped onion, cucumber and garlic (a sort of poor man's *vichysoisse*), then grilled sturgeon, oily, orange and excellent. There was vodka to drink and a rough white wine the tobacco merchant had brought in his pocket.

Before we left ten fishermen ranged themselves before Diana each carrying a very small dog. They wanted her to choose one (or all) as a present and she selected a tiny woolly thing almost too young to take away from its mother (the sad old retriever we had seen on the beach), but so immediately endearing that I consented to its acceptance, consoling myself that its future as a transcontinental traveller could hardly be worse than that of a Black Sea beachcomber. We called it Karrabas, or Black Face, because it had a black face and that is the name most commonly given to big Turkish dogs, like Rover in England. Karrabas took after his father, who was said to be an Anatolian sheepdog, and might therefore develop into a sturdy protector on our travels.

On the way back we rowed out to see if there were any fish caught on the hooks. But the fishermen lifted one row after another, and there was nothing. Here was clearly no place to go investigating under water with a mask: I hoped that the Caspian, the main source of world supply, would offer greater scope to the underwater goggler.

4

ALONG THE BLACK SEA

For two thousand five hundred years the Greeks dominated this Black Sea coast with a chain of commercial colonies. In the unsettled aftermath of the 1914–18 war Venizelos, with Sir Basil Zaharoff lurking somewhere in the background, had dreams of absorbing it into a greater Greek empire. But his 'Great Idea' of *Enosis* at Turkish expense was foiled by Atatürk, who rallied the Turkish people from his headquarters at Ankara, and landing at Samsun began operations that ended in the defeat of the invading Greek army, and the subsequent expulsion of large numbers of Greek residents, the commercial backbone of the coast.

Classical authors, I had decided, would not be my companions on this journey, but I cannot resist a quote from Xenophon's *Anabasis*[1] apropos Giresun, a miserable town about sixty miles from Trabzon (it was from the mountain tops beyond Trabzon that Xenophon's tired Ten Thousand topped the crest and cried, as every schoolboy knows, 'The Sea! The Sea!') outside which we spent the night on a stony beach: In the hills above Giresun, according to Xenophon, lived the barbarian Mossynoici, whose chiefs kept boys 'specially fatted up by being fed on boiled chestnuts. Their flesh was soft and very pale, and they were practically as broad as they were tall. Front and back were brightly coloured all over, tattooed with designs of flowers. These people wanted to have sexual intercourse in public with the mistresses whom the Greeks brought with them, this being actually the normal thing in their country!'

Two entirely undesirable young descendants of the Mossynoici woke us early on their whistling way to school. They stood and stared and would not go away. They wore yachting caps in the manner of most Turkish (and Swedish) scholars, and sported badges with a map of Cyprus. 'KYPRIS—TURKEI! KYPRIS—TURKEI!' they chanted for our benefit, and for the first time in my consideration of that thorny problem I could admit no support at all to their contention.

[1] Trans. Rex Warner. op. cit. Lord Kinross, *Within the Taurus*.

On the outskirts of Trabzon, formerly Trebizond, formerly Trapezus, I found the little church of Saint Sophia perched on a grassy mound above the road. I had been told in Ankara that a team financed by the Walker Trust was surveying afresh this already heavily documented nineteenth-century Byzantine basilica. I particularly wanted to have a look at the frescoes which were then being uncovered by someone called David Winfield. I hoped to find him at work, but sadly, according to one of a group of Turkish youths idling in the fig tree's shade, 'David' was not there. The young man, however, was his assistant and he would be happy to show us the work in progress.

When Patrick Kinross visited the church in 1951 he found it was being used as a military store with drums of oil stacked on the beautiful mosaic floor. The situation had since improved: perhaps with an eye on the tourist trade the Turkish government are tolerant to the icons of the infidel. (The other Saint Sophia, mother of Eastern churches, has been turned into a museum with the original Christian symbols reinstated on the walls; the graceful church of Saint Irene in Istanbul, formerly part of the Sultan's armoury, was being cleaned up and restored when we looked over it.) Now the drums of oil had been removed and the floor of the basilica was more politely covered with carpets. In the centre of the narthex a cross-legged priest sat surlily intoning the *Koran* as if trying to exorcize the images of the unbelievers that were being materialized on the walls before his very eyes. Winfield's assistant led me over to crude wooden scaffolding erected in the choir which I gingerly climbed to inspect the work in progress. The restorers had been laboriously scraping away at the layers of white plaster applied by the Moslem conquerors. 'Peck' marks, hacked in the wall to make the plaster stick, looked like bursts of machine-gun fire, but they could not rob the ancient frescoes of their grandeur. Faces and figures as positive as Giotto's were emerging from the mess, and already 'Doubting Thomas', the 'Virgin Enthroned', and 'Christ and his Disciples on the Sea of Tiberias' appeared again after five centuries of oblivion.

Owing to the non-arrival of the tankers, a frequent occurrence in Turkey, there was no petrol in the Trabzon pumps: if I wanted a special issue I should need a permit from the Chief of Police. His office was shut and we were forced to stay the night in the town. We smuggled Karrabas into the hotel in a briefcase. In the

hall four tough-looking Americans, one of them a negro, were
sprawled round a table playing poker. They barely looked up as
we entered, continuing their game in the offhand manner of
cinematic card players. Trabzon was far from Texas, and I had my
own ideas about what they were doing in that unlikely spot. But
Diana's charms could not divert them from their game and it was
not until the following morning that we managed to establish
contact.

There they were at breakfast, surrounded by their personal
packets of cereals and jars of Maxwell House coffee.

'How like eggy?' the waiter was saying to each in turn,
'Scramble? Sonnysideup?'

A contretemps with Karrabas gave an excuse for conversation:
after a preamble about his breed an angular American asked what
we were doing by the Black Sea. I tried shock tactics and announced that we were spying on the new missile launching sites.
He looked amused rather than shocked and said wryly:

'That's a very explosive subject around here!' He seemed
anxious to change the subject and as he had given us a tin of
condensed milk for Karrabas I thought it polite to drop the
matter.

Beyond Trabzon the hills rose more steeply from the coastal
plain. In the late spring, when we passed that way, the weather
held no hint of the terrible winter winds that whip across the
Black Sea from the Russian north, causing the Greeks to name it
the Axine, or Inhospitable (later Greeks sought to conciliate it
by using the antithesis—Euxine). Now there was a gentle still-
ness, a Celtic softness in the air, compared with which the Mediterranean was harsh and almost garish. Turkey is a land of pines,
but there was not a single conifer in sight upon those softly
deciduous slopes: chestnuts and beech grew among bushes of
hazel; the leafy banks were coloured with wild roses, foxgloves,
honeysuckle, rhododendrons and the Pontic azalea, whose honey
reputedly drives men mad. Little paths led through damp copses
sweet with the smell of bracken, moss and fern. Early one morning I followed a tinkling stream through an orchard of fig and
nut down to a limpid sea. Miniature cyclamen grew at my feet
and wild strawberries, enough to make a breakfast. I came down
to a rocky shore and dived into the cold, clear water.

Approaching Rize the hills became higher and the atmosphere heavier, bluer, more hot-house. The vegetation went through a subtle transmutation: vines and hops and old man's beard now twined around the trees; cypress, citrus, and palm began to stud the slopes, the cold-cream scent of flowering acacia was added to the air. Then another smell became apparent, some fragrant herb, familiar yet unidentifiable. We followed our noses to a large concrete factory, and it was not until I had inspected the huge pile of dried leaves lying in the courtyard that I realized it was tea. We were now in the tea belt and for many miles to come were to see the fields of little dark green bushes, with the lines of women in shawls and dark red and blue striped skirts fussing over them.

At the factory, first of three (four more are to be built) along this stretch of coast, we were taken in hand by a German-speaking Turk who looked deeply hurt when his role as guide was seized by some senior, though less easily understood, member of the staff. This man, who gave a non-stop running commentary in his native tongue, insisted on showing us every facet in the production of a tea leaf and we followed him through drying rooms (with hot air being forced over thinly spread leaves), sorting rooms, grading and packing rooms, and storing rooms. And in each room strange machines whirred and clattered and shuttled, with names like 'Rigid Rapid Roller (Double Action)' and 'Britannia Made Pucca Tea Sorter (Made in India)'. At last we came out the other end, practically wrapped up in packets ourselves, and took tea with the management on the balcony of a little villa in the grounds. Before leaving we were presented with a pound of 'Rize Orange Pekoe'.

Tea is the vital crop along this stretch of coast and its recent introduction has brought new life to a district that was dying piecemeal of economic anaemia. Like Trabzon, Rize was commercially dependant on Russia, sending her sons to work there (whence they returned when they had made their fortune) and selling her staple product, fruit, in Batum. But after the Russian revolution Rize became like a head without a body. Then in the 1920s the Russians found that the eastern end of the Black Sea was suitable for growing tea, but it was not for fifteen years that it occurred to the Turks it also might be possible to grow tea along their coast. A man of Rize went to Ceylon and Darjeeling to study cultivation and largely as a result of his efforts the district now produces 2,500 tons, fifty per cent of the Turkish consumption. The other fifty per cent, which is mixed in with the local growth, is largely of British origin.

In the high street of Rize we met an English-speaking citizen who offered to take us up the hill to the *fidanlik*, or 'place of little trees', the terraced garden where the original tea-growing experiments had been made. As we had to wait until the petrol tanker arrived we were happy to follow him up the steep cobbled path that climbed the exotic hillside.

Down below the red roofs of Rize glowed in the setting sun. A line of tea-laden caiques was casting off for the long coastal run to Istanbul. The evening air was heavy with the scent of roses and lemon blossom. An eastern songstress ululated distantly: Violetta's theme song from *Traviata* would have been more in keeping with that sadly romantic setting.

Our guide was a supplier of builders' materials. Returning to the town, he took us to the so-called *Kasino*, a restaurant-café by the sea, large and bare as a railway station, where we ate salted pistachio nuts and drank soda pop and met some of his friends, the younger professional set of Rize. We were invited to stay the night, but preferred the open air and slept instead under the stars within a few feet of the gently surging sea.

Eastwards from Rize tobacco began to alternate with the tea gardens along the coastal strip, the firm yet delicate green leaves of the young plants projecting confidently from the central stalk, an attractive crop even for a non-smoker. Behind, the hills were now reaching higher and sometimes, through gaps in their façade, more serious snow-capped peaks stood out, meriting the appelation 'Dag' on the map. Occasional conifers now appeared and the brightly-shawled peasants on their early morning way to market carried wooden objects for sale—gaily painted babies' cradles on rockers, baskets and little wheeled carts—indicating they were a mountain people, craftsmen in wood. The women were shy and hid their faces in their shawls at our approach or turned into the ditch and looked the other way. But sometimes they introduced a gesture that expressed not so much shyness as a rude resentment that we—infidels? under-dressed? unveiled? or merely the masculine me?—should presume to pass that way.

Soon we came to Hopa—little more than a petrol pump, a

barracks, a broken down quay once used for loading copper, and a disintegration of wooden houses. Hopa, according to our small scale tourist map, was the end of the coastal road. About twenty miles beyond, perhaps over that hazy headland curving out to sea, was the enormous bulk of Soviet Russia.

5

ACROSS THE TAURUS

FRONTIERS have for me a romantic appeal greater than their actual significance. I admit to a vicarious thrill even on approaching a friendly one. Thus I felt a mounting excitement when, meeting with no challenge at Hopa, we continued confidently, though bumpily, towards Russia.

The road became ruder and narrower and soon began to curve inland, crossing a steep pass that gave a magnificent view over terraced tea-gardens newly claimed from the forested slopes. According to my map the road should have turned in a southerly direction, but it suddenly wheeled back to the sea and clung to the coast again. We passed some soldiers working on a field telephone, who regarded us quizzically but made no attempt to stop the car. We continued through a small village, reassured by children playing in the road, and about a mile further on came to a large army truck parked across the track in a gateway. Curving up through the conifers beyond I could see an earthen road which I hoped would take us into Artvin by the back door. I squeezed the car through a narrow gap and, meeting no challenge from the nearby concrete blockhouse, drove confidently across the open space ahead.

I had gone about fifty yards when there was an urgent shouting behind. Wondering whether to go on or stop, a decision was forced on me by the car, which stuck in a gully and would not immediately move forwards. Struggling with the four-wheel-drive mechanism we were surrounded by a troop of soldiers who prodded us with rifles and frantically signalled us to return the way we had come.

In front of the blockhouse a map of Turkey made of pebbles bore the legend VATAN—Fatherland. Slit-eyed soldiers peered suspiciously through barred windows and embrasures. A stocky sergeant hurried towards us and jabbed his finger upwards into the trees. In the wood, about a hundred and fifty yards away, stood a tall wooden tower with a boxlike platform on top. Two men could be seen looking from it in our direction.

'Soviet Rusya! Soviet Rusya!' hissed the sergeant, pointing eastwards and I suddenly saw what had happened and appreciated our good fortune at being stopped. This blockhouse was the eastern limit of Turkey. We had crossed into No-Man's-Land and the earth road I had witlessly planned to take was in fact the ploughed strip that invariably defines a Russian frontier—kept well-hoed to show the footprints of fly-by-nights and no doubt sewn with mines as well. If that friendly gully had not stopped us it was a nice speculation who would have shot at us first—the Turks as escapees or the Russians as invaders.

The phlegmatic Turkish sergeant seemed to accept my explanation, expressed in terms of pointing at the map and scratching my head in bewilderment, that I had in error taken the wrong road. After all, an odd-looking man in jeans and a schoolboy's yachting cap and a girl in a pale blue sack dress accompanied by a little dog called Karrabas could hardly be suspected of any really sinister intent. Nevertheless he mounted a guard over us—four stalwart soldiers with scruffy uniforms and stubbly chins, but proud in their bearing and determined in their stance. We waited impatiently in their company while messages were sent back to determine our future.

After a time we were moved back to the village and sat under a walnut tree while various people had a go at asking questions. The village schoolmaster, who clearly had a reputation as an English speaker to maintain, was the first to try and though we did our best to help him little headway could be made. Then some civilian authority, perhaps a *kaimakam*, appeared, together with a major and an elderly colonel. My passport was passed from hand to hand and heavy eyebrows were raised when it was seen to contain several Iron Curtain visas from previous travels.

'You speak Russian?' the major asked, setting a weighty trap. My reply of 'Niet!' did not amuse him.

But the atmosphere was friendly. Everybody tried out their little bit of English. The '*kaimakam*' was an admirer of Princess Margaret. He thought it 'very bad' of the 'Pope of London' to interfere in her marriage plans. 'Very bad' was a favourite idiom of his:

'Soviet Rusya very bad!' he said, apropos of nothing.

'Am I very bad?' I asked, meaning to sound out the attitude of the authorities to my presence there.

'No. You are very good. I like you very much,' he replied disarmingly.

Difficult conversation continued for some hours and it was not clear how the situation was ever going to resolve itself. At last a jeep arrived from Hopa containing a young captain wearing an American-style uniform. He spoke fairly fluent American having, he told us, served with the Turkish contingent in Korea and afterwards on a liaison job in Japan. When I had told my story once again he pointed out that the road was 'off limits' after Hopa, but he could not deny that there was no notice to this effect. A second jeep now arrived bearing a dark, thickset man with Asian eyes. It was my guess that he belonged to the secret police.

The captain said that if I wanted to go to Iran I should now have to return to Trabzon and thence take the main road to Erzurum. This was the edict I had been dreading, for apart from disappointing my publisher it would add another two days to my journey. I protested and pleaded. After conferring with the newly-arrived civilian the latter jumped into his jeep.

'Follow, please!' he said, and not knowing what was in store for us we roared off after him.

When he did not stop at Hopa, but turned inland beyond it, I felt that there was still a chance that we might not after all be sent back to Trabzon in disgrace. We played follow my leader—and our leader was difficult to keep up with—over high fantastic passes and down into magic misty valleys. The sun went down behind distant snow-peaks and we dropped steeply into darkness. The jeep was waiting for us at the end of a long iron bridge guarded by a soldier with a fixed bayonet. We followed across rushing moon-flecked water and turned into a courtyard beside a large wooden house.

I expected some sort of a police station and was pleasantly surprised to find myself in a room decorated with such familiar objects as family photographs, bright silk cushions and elaborately dressed celluloid dolls. A motherly lady greeted us and patting Diana kindly, suggested she might like to wash. A complicated piece of ironmongery in a cupboard produced the first hot water we had seen in a week and after we had wiped the accumulated filth of travel on her clean white towels our hostess led us on to a wooden balcony where she had laid out a spread of

bread, cherry jam, honey, chocolate cake, olives, cheese and tea.
The moon now shone through jagged clouds revealing an expanse
of fiercely churning water just below. It was the river Çoruh
(pronounced 'Chorra'), which must have been dammed below the
bridge to form that boiling lake. Thence it rushed on down into
Russia, finally forming the harbour of Batum. This place we
learned, was Borcka.

We were joined at tea by a pale young girl, who was introduced
as an English speaker, but this could not be confirmed as she was
too shy to open her mouth. I was anxious to know what authority our host had in that region and learned that he was 'Chief
Intelligent Officer', a status I had not previously encountered.
I confess I then suspected his hospitality had the secondary purpose
of holding us up until clearance had been obtained from some
higher authority. Indeed, he disappeared to answer a telephone
and returned shortly afterwards to tell us that we might continue
on our way through Artvin, but were on no account to take the
road through Ardahan and Kars. This was certainly better than
returning to Trabzon, and I gladly undertook not to stray from
the route. He warned us that the road ahead was dangerous and
advised us to spend the night at Borcka. But we wanted to be on
our way and having said good-bye to his kindly wife and been
seen across the bridge and past the guard, drove off into the
darkness.

The fitful moon soon revealed the undoubted hazards of the
way. We had climbed above the river and now clung to the sides
of a great gorge. The road was steep and narrow and crossed with
subsidences that tended to wrench the wheels towards the edge.
I nervously pulled off into the first ravine I came to and we slept
beside a rushing stream that fled towards the great river in the
gorge below. Looking up at the rocky skyline it was as if great
bears and hooded *penitentes* were peering down on us. But the
dawn revealed them as twisted fir trees and our Magnasco visions
were replaced by a friendlier picture of yellow-breasted wagtails
hopping on the boulders of the stream, fringed with red flowering
shrubs and the familiar valerian of Devon banks.

By seven the sun was already hot and shining happily on the
Armenian town of Artvin, perched on the hillside high above the
gorge. It was the prettiest town I had seen in Turkey, with red
roofs and white walls and minarets and pale green poplars and the

Çoruh river swirling darkly far below. We looked down on a miniature army camp with matchbox military vehicles disposed on the parade ground—big five-ton American lorries, toylike jeeps, and ambulances marked with the Red Crescent.

We took a wrong turning outside the town and might have continued to Ardahan had I not felt that it would be an abuse of Turkish hospitality and forbearance to disobey instructions. Instead we turned back and descended like good children into the valley of the Çoruh. We were soon swallowed up in an enormous deep-cut gorge through which the Tiber-brown river rushed with formidable vigour. Now the jagged purplish hills were bare except for stunted junipers whose twisted roots could often be seen swirling down the river to end, if not intercepted at Borcka, perhaps on the beach at Batum.

In the hot mid-morning we were held up by a fall of rock across the road. Clearance was proceeding in a very leisurely manner and we took the advice of a tractor driver, similarly delayed, to retire to a nearby orchard, where coloured rugs and cushions had been laid out in the approved Oriental manner. We disported ourselves gratefully in the shade and awaited only a slave girl to bring us sherbet and grapes. Instead an old man appeared with a basket of a whitish fruit, sweet and very refreshing. He called it *tut* and pointed out how it grew on the trees all around. It was, in fact, a sort of mulberry, but quite unlike the fat, rank English version of that delectable Eastern fruit. Pomegranates, too, would have been appropriate fare in that enchanted spot, but the many spiky bushes that bore them showed no more at that time of year than red trumpet-shaped flowers.

Other disgruntled travellers joined us under the trees and we should probably have remained there all day had I not learned from a lorry driver that it was possible to get to Erzurum by crossing the river a mile or two higher up and taking the road through Tortum. This was not strictly according to the directions given me at Borcka but there seemed no other reasons against it. After a stimulating dip in the river, effected by clinging to rocks on the bank and letting the stream swirl past me, an exercise which horrified the onlookers, we retraced our route to the bridge and followed the opposite bank.

Tortum contained nothing of interest, but beyond we came to a great reservoir. Electric pylons led away towards Erzurum but as yet there were no wires to carry the still uncreated current. The hills were now levelling out into a grassy plain. Pillboxes cut in the rock with significant fields of fire up the valley informed us that we were in invasion territory. Down in the plain we passed many barracks and concentrations of transport and artillery. Sentries, wearing white gloves and lanyards and the tin hat of the British Tommy (made to look even less potent by the addition of rings of red and white paint), waved us urgently past every side road and likely entrance. Before long we were entering the sleazy outskirts of an Eastern Aldershot.

6

FRONTIER INCIDENT

THE NATURAL fortress of Erzurum is, in Turkish eyes, the linchpin of their defence against Russian incursions from Asia. In the last two hundred years it has been attacked in four wars and captured in three. It held out in the Russo–Turkish war of 1877 if only because the Russians were more actively engaged in approaching Constantinople via Bulgaria.

Turkey has over half a million men under arms. At least one-third of them are based on Erzurum; Erzurum is 'army', and I knew that foreigners travelling through were required to take on a military escort whose duty was to prevent the unmasking of the secrets of Turkish defence. I did not know, however, where this ritual 'taking on' was enacted and cruised around among the many soldiers in the town only too anxious to be boarded. I finally gathered from a Swedish traveller at a petrol pump that the performance took place at Pasinlar.

The hotels of Erzurum were uninviting, even sinister. Deciding not to stay we drove out past mysterious monuments, battered latticed houses, sidewalk officers' clubs, and the decrepit trappings of an Asian emporium, to the open country beyond. We continued until we were tired and spent the night by the roadside.

Morning revealed a bare plain, which on closer investigation was less bare than we had imagined, for it was strewn with military obstacles masquerading as natural objects. Ditches were tank traps, haystacks masked concrete pillboxes, tumbledown barns disguised strong points, and the most humble mound was likely to contain a meaningful slit. There now seemed no question of a military escort for we were out of the zone and had unwittingly passed through Pasinlar in the night. Trying not to look too interested in our surroundings we came to Karaköse in time for breakfast.

Over tea and cheese in a café we were joined by two friendly traffic policemen, who proudly demonstrated the mechanism of their newly issued pistols. In return I showed them my Luger, smuggled into Turkey in the tool-box, which was much admired. Then we drove on.

Mount Ararat appeared: first as a snow-white hump playing hide-and-seek with the horizon, then suddenly revealing itself unreservedly over the skyline, a rock-strewn base topped by a snow-capped cone. Jonquils, gentians and stunted irises with petals of an evil velvety brown grew in the turfy fields. A man was doing something peculiar in a ditch, urgently plunging his arms into the black mud. As we watched he drew up a large fish, which he proudly displayed to us. It must have come up there to spawn, perhaps from the far Euphrates via the nearby Murat.

At Doubayazid, about forty miles from the frontier, we were stopped by a booted policeman wearing an American-style hexagonal cap. He refused to return our papers, saying that orders had come through by telephone that we were to be detained. He did not seem to know the reason and I began to wonder if my childish behaviour in comparing my illicit Luger with the pistols of the traffic police was about to meet its just retribution. Or was it simply that I had left my hat behind in the café and they were trying to let me know? The latter speculation gave me the idea of telling the policeman that I knew that I had been stopped because the police at Karaköse kindly wished to return my hat; as I did not want my hat, could we please continue our journey? It is not often that Turkish simplicity exceeds Turkish suspiciousness, but much to my surprise the policeman accepted this explanation and allowed us to pass.

While these negotiations were in progress a crowded lorry had drawn up and from the hurly-burly of men, women, babies and animals in the back a tall bony figure extricated himself and came over towards us. His face was windblown, his sprouting beard was clogged with sand; he wore a pale blue ski jacket, wide khaki trousers kept from flapping by bicycle clips, and enormous hobnailed boots; the leather belt round his waist was stuck with a variety of knives and bullets. His first words—'Can I be of any help?'—were not necessary for me to guess that he was an Englishman, a notable specimen of that type of traveller who has somewhere to get to and is prepared to go there 'hard'. His name was Tony and his destination was India. His transport, now in the lorry, was a push-bike with a tiny waspish Italian engine fitted. He had broken down somewhere in the middle of Anatolia and was trying to get to Teheran, where spare parts were being sent by post. We felt we ought to offer him a lift but it was hot and we were out of temper, and Karrabas needed room: he would be better off in his bus. So we said light-heartedly, 'See you at the frontier', and drove away before the policeman changed his mind.

It did not seem long before we reached the arch that marked the entrance to the Turkish–Iranian Customs. We passed through into a courtyard bounded on four sides by administrative buildings. A barrier ran across the middle patrolled on either side by the soldiers of the respective countries.

In the courtyard we found ourselves in the middle of a group of army officers. They wore the uniforms of several nations and stood around in the expectant attitude of a party of Cook's tourists. Seeing a British colonel in crisp battle-dress, I asked him what was going on. He told me they were from NATO headquarters at Izmir, and were touring the frontier areas. I said that I hoped to visit Izmir (formerly Smyrna) on my return journey, whereupon he handed me his card and suggested I pay him a call there. I read that his name was Lunn-Rockcliffe and I was suddenly able to place him as a freckle-faced, curly-haired boy with whom I had been at school. We had barely established this lowest common factor when a large Turkish policeman, wearing a big-badged cap, a revolver-slung blue jacket, black breeches and soft leather boots that crinkled like a concertina, darted forwards and grabbed the colonel's card from my hand. Then he seized the keys of the car and some miscellaneous papers Diana was carrying.

This surprising behaviour angered me so much that when he refused to return them I tried to regain possession by force, seizing him by the arm and prizing open his fingers. An ugly little 'frontier incident' was now developing. I tried to make the issue centre round the rape of the colonel's card. Had not a British officer, representative of a NATO power (how eager the Turks had been to join!) been equally insulted by having his card so rudely confiscated? If they thought I was a spy communicating with another spy then *ipso facto* they were suggesting that the NATO colonel was a spy! There was something to be said for this argument and a Turkish brigadier now rather testily intervened. As a result the card was returned and the NATO commitment correspondingly reduced.

The NATO contingent now withdrew with cries of 'Good Luck!' from the English-speaking element.

The plump policeman came into his own again and ordered me to remain where I was. A shiny Mercedes charabanc came through from the Persian side and I looked for support among its occupants. A depraved-looking Iranian who spoke some English having been attached to the American forces, and a Japanese youth slung with cameras now befriended us.

I asked the Iranian to inquire why I was being held. But apparently the policeman did not know: there had been a telephone call and he must wait for further instructions. Then, conspiratorially, in an undertone, the Iranian hissed a sinister question:

'You are not perhaps carrying some opium?'

When the hateful policeman conveyed to me that I would have to return to Doubayazid, I realized that this was the second chapter of the previous effort to detain us. There was nothing for it, since my protests were utterly ignored, but to return the fiery forty miles to the grim dust trap we had so thankfully quitted some three hours earlier.

'Everything OK in Iran!' said the Persian, consolingly. 'Plenty Pepsi. Plenty everything.'

Our position became no happier at Doubayazid. A rat-faced *chef de gendarmerie* with a sly eye emerged from his concrete police station escorted by his small force of three gendarmes and ordered us to wait outside. We waited. After an hour of standing in the sun, wooden chairs were brought. Six incipient poplars, mere poles stuck in the ground, provided no shade. A soldier, a Mongol-featured youth armed with a .45 automatic, was now put on guard over us. Time passed. Miscellaneous villagers shuffled across the dusty square to get a closer look. A bearded brute gave Karrabas, who was lying unhappily but harmlessly in the sun, a vicious kick. This set Diana off and she gave an even harder kick to his tormentor. Occasional Kurds in their Victorian ragbag dress shuffled listlessly by. A bus named 'INSHALLAH' drew up nearby and a fight developed between the driver and a Turkish Teddy who had knocked off his cap. The widow Ararat gloomed disapprovingly down on our left.

Then a familiar figure stalked across the square. It was Tony, the bearded Englishman, whose lorry could carry him no further. 'Can I be of any help?' he asked once again. He was not allowed to be for a policeman chased him away and would not let us communicate.

We had been there for about six hours, offered neither tea nor sympathy. Nobody would say what was happening. We were angry and exhausted. Then at last a jeep arrived, the smart 'Utility' model, and an elderly man got out and hurried into the gendarmerie without a glance in our direction. Then another car drew up and a tall man in a light khaki uniform and bright brown cavalry boots stepped out. There was red and gold around his cap. He was a general.

After a further wait we were summoned into the building and came before an inquisition assembled round a table. The general, who looked like Julius Caesar, explained in formal English that he was attending simply as an interpreter and that the inquiry was being conducted by civilian authorities. Then, through this distinguished intermediary, the questioning began and the answers were taken down in longhand. First an inquiry about parentage to the nth generation and places of residence since birth.

'Do you have relations with this woman?' the general asked curtly, nodding towards Diana, and I was framing an embarrassed reply when he added: 'I mean is she of your family?'

Then came a series of questions about our route—Had I taken any photographs? Had I seen the reservoir at Tortum? Why had I gone through Erzurum without an escort?—The substance of the case against me was now clear: I had not taken the exact route specified by the Intelligence Officer at Borcka, who had apparently telephoned through to Erzurum. I had not reported to the police at Erzurum (I had not been told to) and I had not taken on a military escort (none had been offered). Apparently my arrival from the north instead of the west had enabled me to pass the military checkpoint. The Swede's information about Pasinlar was in any case superfluous because that was the checkpoint for travellers coming from the other direction.

My answers must have satisfied them that I was not a spy, for the general made a short speech apologizing for our detention and explaining that 'the dangerous enemy to the north' made it necessary to take the strongest security precautions. I replied with a formal little speech of my own suggesting that in future the police should handle bona fide travellers with more consideration.

'I hope you will not write about these things," said the general.

Nor perhaps would I have done, had it not been for the further infuriating delay at the frontier.

There was the plump Turkish policeman of the morning looking very pleased with himself and at our discomfort, and making no effort to pass us through. When I protested at the hold-up I was told that the officials concerned were having their supper. When the Customs men had finally done their job they said that the man who stamped the *carnet* had gone to see his sick mother. These delaying tactics lasted for an hour. Why did I not stay the night? they asked sarcastically. I could sleep in the car under the shelter.

This was too much. I was determined not to spend another night in Turkey. I made the gesture of stripping off the police-man's badges of rank at the same time shouting 'Ankara! Ankara!' to indicate that I intended to complain to the highest authority in the land. At this all the Customs men spat with a concerted spit. Spitting is a widespread and detestable habit in Turkey and I spat back with added venom.

The Persian Customs, anxious to pack up for the night, were following every move from the other side of the barrier. They encouraged the argument with their own interpolations, which I sensed were in our favour. Finally, after I had sounded my horn for several ear-piercing seconds, with the threat of continuing indefinitely, the Turks decided to call it a day.

Swallows were nesting under the eaves of the Iranian Customs House. The Persians were kind, they were quick and they were not too conscientious. On the understanding that we were carry-ing no bacon or pigs' fat, saffron, angelica, red pepper, assafoetida, opium, hashish, henbane, alcoholic drinks, immoral pictures and prints, 'all kinds of soap for washing', not to mention portable firearms and their parts, we were through in a few minutes.

'Ils sont des bêtes, là bas!' said a sleek Persian, with a shake of his head towards the Turkish Customs. Just then I was inclined to agree.

7

TABRIZ

FIVE MILES inside Persia we came upon Tony, the bearded Englishman, wearily trundling his bicycle up a hill. It now seemed an appropriate moment to offer him a lift. We strapped his bicycle on to the car's flat bonnet, but when I tried to hoist his bulging rucksack I found I could barely lift it off the ground. Tony, however, tossed it lightly aboard and explained how he had designed it so that it could also be fitted on to the back of a horse. He must have been as strong as a horse himself.

Our new passenger, as might have been deduced from such references as the 'high bacterial content' of the water and the 'vitamin deficiency' in the local diet, was a science teacher. He had taught in a secondary school near London; his pupils were 'an insubordinate lot of monkeys' by his account, to whom discipline had sometimes to be instilled with a spank. This, to Tony's disgust, was discouraged by the authorities. Now he was forsaking the restrictions of Hounslow for the great spaces of the Himalayas. He had a bold and interesting plan to cross the northern part of Nepal from east to west, that is against the grain of the country, over innumerable rivers and ridges and through hitherto unpenetrated forests peopled by tribes who were known not to welcome visitors. Tony had been planning this one-man expedition for the past two years and if anybody gets through that deadly territory it will be him. My thoughts are with him now, as armed with his big knife against hostile animals, his skill at jujitsu against unfriendly natives, and a little red book called *A Manual of Tropical Medicine* against sickness and snake-bites, he crashes onwards through the jungle. Tony confided that he also hoped to meet and photograph an Abominable Snowman and I like to think of the two of them comparing notes deep in the mountains of Nepal.

We stopped for the night by the wayside and Tony cooked us an omelette, with a judicious addition of flour 'to make it go further'. By 'living off the land', eating with the peasants and sleeping in his little orange nylon tent he had spent under £10

since leaving England. Almost all his capital had gone on equip-
ping himself for the great journey, leaving only too little to
accomplish it. He had hoped to raise additional finance by writing
articles about his travels for local newspapers, but his experience in Turkey had been that far from paying him for his contribution they expected him to pay for its insertion. However, he
had managed to sell some of his blood to an Istanbul hospital,
for which he had been paid 50 lira. 'About half what they pay in
Beirut!' he complained. Tony looked very thin as he crept into
his little tent and I advised him to save all his blood for the long
journey that lay ahead.

Little has been said in this narrative about our sleeping
arrangements. I had bought a beautiful circular tent in London,
guaranteed insect-proof, with tubular rubber ribs that when
inflated gave it the appearance of an ample igloo. It was no fault
of the tent that we rarely used it, but of the car pump, which did
not seem able to introduce enough air into the ribs to make it
stand up. My occasional efforts, after a gruelling day's drive,
proved so ruinous to my temper that after a time I gave it up
and we took to sleeping in the open on the ground or, in bad
weather and insect-haunted spots, in the back and front of the car
respectively.

There is vast excitement in camping in the dark and waking
early not knowing what you will see around you. I thought we
had shaken her off but to my surprise Ararat, shawled in snow,
still watched over us, her stony base straddling three countries—
Russia, Turkey and Persia. To the right was Little Ararat, smaller
than her mother and snowless, part of Persia until 1930, a strong-
hold of rebel Turkish Kurds; after the Kurdish revolt it was
exchanged with the Turks for some land further south.

Tony brewed some tea and an old Kurdish shepherd gravely
watched the proceedings. Karrabas investigated his goats with
interest under the impression they were dogs.

We had our first impression of a Persian interior when we
stopped at a tea house, where Tony, who had already acquired
a working knowledge of Turkish, the basic language in the west
of Persia, professionally ordered bread and yoghourt and showed
us the correct method of scooping up the curdled milk with the
flat *chupatti* bread. In the corner of the simple room, under
coloured prints of the Shah and Soraya (in dark glasses), a samovar

was steaming and glasses (smaller than we were used to in Turkey)
were filled with tea and emptied many times before we continued
on our way. The ubiquitous *chai khanas*, or tea houses, were to be
our mainstay and comfort over the many miles that lay ahead.

The Persian countryside, though lacking the grandeur of the
Turkish uplands, possessed a more formal elegance. We found a
grove of poplars for a picnic beyond Khoi and while eating
watched a string of small green taxis driving past, apparently for
the fun of it, with wirelesses playing loudly. They were a Russian
make called 'Moskvitch' and were, I imagine, part of a newly
arrived consignment from the north which the proud owners
were putting through their paces. They had almost certainly
entered the country via Julfa, where the Russian railway system
linked up with the line to Tabriz. Armed with the necessary
permits, I hoped to take a look at Julfa on my return.

Orchards and irrigation were soon swallowed up in a salty
desert that was almost continually with us to Tabriz. I was
chasing sandgrouse and observing their zigzag, almost snipe-like
flight, when the car door flew open and Karrabas, who had been
lying in his favourite position by the accelerator pedal, fell out
on to the stony ground. He lay inert in the dust and when I
picked him up gave no sign of life. I thought his little odyssey
was over, when he opened a bleeding eye, gave a puzzled grunt,
and began to lick my hand. By the time we reached Tabriz he was
his old self—the Tiny Turk, gruff, independent and irrepressible.

The best hotel in Tabriz is the Metropole, a modernistic concrete
building next door to a cinema which on the day of our arrival
was showing Ava Gardner in *Fire Down Below*. Tony said he did
not have enough money to stay in an hotel and wanted to camp
somewhere in the town. He was apparently used to civic camping.
Once, he told us, he had pitched his tent in the public square of
Caetan. While he was getting things straight a large crowd of
Sicilians collected to watch the performance. When he had
installed himself they kept poking their heads inside to have a
look at the odd *Inglese*. Tony, from within, had reasoned with
them:

'This is my home. How would you feel if people came and
looked at you in *your* house?' His argument had appealed to the
home-loving Italians and they had gone away and left him in

peace. But I could not see an Iranian crowd reacting in the same way, and I persuaded him to stay at the hotel by offering to pay for his room.

The Metropole dining-room laid claims to be the social centre of the town. Its walls were of concrete sprayed with green and gold enlivened by Coca-Cola calendars and sylvan landscapes and fruit still-lifes mechanically reproduced to look like oil-paintings; jazz-age chandeliers hung from the ceiling; in the corner a three-piece band was playing nostalgic tunes from the repertoire of Central Europe. The musicians were to match—an ageing Lupescu-like redhead at the piano, a soulful virtuoso on the violin, and an elderly man on the drums (surely a former prime minister of some Balkan state).

There was something appropriately bizarre about the diners. At the next table was a depraved-looking party I put down as international dope smugglers—women in trousers, with dyed blonde hair, cigarettes drooping from lascivious mouths, and *maquereaux*-like men with weak chins and fancy American shirts of outrageous design. At another table Erich von Stroheim was dining alone and to attention. Across the room a group of dark-suited men, one with a pointed beard, were huddled in con-spiratorial discussion. The only unsinister figures were a clean-cut young man in a dinner-jacket and his companion, a matronly lady with her hair done in tight little curls, wearing a bright green taffeta dress. The unravelling of identities was effected through their agency. The young man was Mr Thomas, American vice-consul, and the lady a cultural import from America, a harpist who had that evening given a recital to the music lovers of Tabriz and would shortly be repeating the performance in Teheran. The band, apparently, were Russian *émigrés* from Armenia; the drug fiends were Spanish dancers; Erich von Stroheim was a Swedish agricultural expert; and the conspirators were two members of the Russian Trade Mission doing business with an Iranian im-porter. After this comprehensive cataloguing the American vice-consul bravely and gaily took the harpist for a dance and we settled down to bortsch, chicken and rice, Coca-Cola and Russian tea.

Next morning we 'did' Tabriz. There was something peacefully provincial about the place. Though the second largest city in Iran and the capital of Persian Azerbidjan it seemed to doze behind the

dun mud walls that lined the suburban streets. The centre indeed
had shops with flashy façades; and bulbous buses (marvellously
coloured viridian, lilac, ginger, fuchsia, magenta); and handsome
government buildings; and a chocolate-mould statue of the Shah.
But life seemed geared to the pace of the decrepit *droshkies* that
sagged forlornly under the plane trees. This caused the more
ambitious citizens to complain that they were being left out of
things and that all the cash and the Cadillacs went to Teheran.
The recent opening by the Shah of a new railway to the capital
should give them hope of better things to come, and further
sunder Azerbidjan's traditional spirit of separatism from the
central authority.

With Marco Polo in mind we strolled through the covered
bazaar, inspecting the unfamiliar substances displayed—the crude
sugar, the dried fruits, the cheeses, the obscure cuts of meat, the
innumerable varieties of nuts. There were carpet shops, and shops
full of cotton material, apparently of Russian manufacture, for a
trade mark depicting the Kremlin was stamped upon the bolts.
As compared with Turkey Tabriz was well stocked with goods,
the most popular item of the new consumer age being apparently
the sewing machine. A whole street was given over to their
display, mostly machines of Japanese origin, ornately decorated
in the rococo style of the cigar box, and bearing such Occidental
names as BRIDE, WOMAN, EAGLE. Equally Occidental were the
names of their Oriental manufacturers—Berkely Mfg Co., Brook-
field Mfg Co. and the like.

I was on the look out for indications of those separatist ten-
dencies that have characterized the recent history of Tabriz.
During the last war Azerbidjan was in the Russian zone of occupation, and what the Russians hold they do not give up lightly.
They used their occupation to engineer a Communist rebellion in
Tabriz, as a result of which, in December 1945, the 'Autonomous
Government of Azerbidjan' was established, a Russian puppet
independent of the central government in Teheran. A companion
régime was established in Kurdistan to the south.

When the Russians failed to evacuate Iran in March 1946
according to treaty obligations, a major international scare was
on and for a time there was a possibility of war between Russia
and the West. Then suddenly, for reasons which are not entirely
clear, the Russians abandoned their protégés, and when the

Shah's troops moved in from Teheran, made no effort to support the military force they had created. Suddenly, after a year of existence, the 'Autonomous Government of Azerbidjan' and the 'Peoples' Republic of Kurdistan' came to a sorry end, and rows of rebels swung ignominiously from the gibbet.

I asked an Armenian silk dealer in the bazaar, who might reasonably be expected to be impartial except where his trading position was concerned, whether he thought Tabriz would ever again favour a Russian occupation.

'They are chameleons, here,' he said equivocally. 'When it is red'—he picked up a red ballpoint—'they are red. When it is green'—he prodded a green plastic ashtray—'they are green.'

The only British representation in Tabriz was the recently opened British Council, known locally as Sura-ye-farang-e-Britania. I had left this as a forwarding address and went round to collect mail. I found it with some difficulty in a pleasant backstreet building, surprisingly capacious behind an unpromising mud wall. In an office by the library and reading room on the first floor I met the Director, Mr Popplestone, a headmasterly-mannered man, as indeed he was, having previously run a school in Kabul. He asked if I had ever had measles, since his eight-year-old son was suffering from them, and when I said I had, kindly invited me to lunch.

The Popplestones lived at the back of the building which overlooked a vineyard and vegetable garden. Mrs Popplestone was an active lady, well equipped to help her husband with his work, having once been County Librarian in Morecambe, Lancs. Grace was said before lunch (I sat down prematurely) and ginger ale was drunk, my hosts being TT, no great social disadvantage in a Moslem country.

Apparently there was much enthusiasm in Tabriz for learning English. French used to be the favoured second language, but now all the schoolchildren plough through the 'Direct Method' and their elders patronize Mr Popplestone. Over three hundred had signed on during the short time he had been there, paying 600 rials for a three months' course. Two members of the Russian Purchasing Mission had presented themselves as aspirants, but Mr Popplestone suspected it was some sort of plot and was glad that his official terms of reference—to represent British Culture to the Iranians—could reasonably be argued to exclude other nationalities.

After lunch we visited the sickroom of Master Popplestone, and Mrs Popplestone read him some Enid Blyton (or similar) to keep him quiet. I felt some anxiety when I remembered it was *German* measles I had had.

On Mr Popplestone's recommendation we left the stuffy town to visit a popular park a few miles outside. Being *Jumma*, the citizens were out in force to picnic under the trees. Under long lines of fig and pistachio veiled women sat huddled round their private samovars attended by their children but deserted by their menfolk, who made noisy groups of their own. We stopped to watch a dynamic group who were dancing frenetically to the music of lute and drum. They came out in turn into the circle and measured their skill in a *pas seul*, weaving and waving their bodies about in a highly unmasculine manner. The winner was certainly a soldier who did a sort of sword dance around his bayonet, bobbing back and forth and grinning, finally doffing his cap to Diana as he came to a panting finish.

In the middle of the park was a large expanse of water with a pavilion on an island in the middle, like a topless Taj Mahal. Near the entrance there was a congregation of cafés, competing for trade by the display of colourful bottles on the tables. It was now brought home to us that we had entered the Soft Drink Belt —the land of Pepsi-Cola, Coca-Cola, O-So, and Canada Dry. (The Turks, handicapped by restrictions, could only offer an inferior local imitation called Kola Koka.) These American 'beverages', brewed and bottled in the country, became the welcome palliatives of our dusty progress almost to the borders of Afghanistan, where the Cola Trail regrettably petered out. In every village along the route these to-us-desirable drinks were sold by the roadside, often miraculously iced. The price to a foreigner might go as high as ten rials, but they would accept six if you insisted. Diana and I drank at least a dozen bottles a day. The number of bottles sold in Iran is astronomical. The soft drink trade must be one of the main bulwarks against Communism, for every salesman is a capitalist trading his way to the top.

Tabriz has little to offer the average tourist. The only item of interest was the Blue Mosque which, though venerable, is disappointing to the unscholarly, being almost derelict, a crumbling dome with most of the blue tiles missing and a courtyard filled with enormous slabs of alabaster. We were met on the threshold by a schoolmaster who ran the school next door. At Tony's request he invited us to look over it.

It was a boys' school and in the classrooms shaven-headed scholars in Victorian black smocks were learning their lessons with fanatical application. The headmaster called forward his star pupil, a little boy of twelve who bowed gravely and made a solemn speech of welcome. In the break the staff of four were introduced and Tony really came into his own, trading technical information about 'school leaving ages' and 'primary and secondary education' in England for illiteracy figures in Iran (which seemed to be as much as 80 per cent) and their current shortage of school buildings and qualified teachers (improving fast).

I was to see another school before I left Tabriz, run by Mme Zand, the Governor-General's wife, out of funds from Queen Soraya's Charity. It was for orphans and unwanted children and I was greatly moved by the way it was conducted—the clean schoolrooms, the sympathetic teachers, and the charming children in mulberry smocks, who sang me a metallic little non-separatist song about their 'Father the Shah'.

8

TEHERAN

THIRTY MILES from Teheran, at Khasvin, we stopped for a Coca-Cola and were joined by a Persian schoolmaster. Tony had now switched his studies from Turkish to Farsi (Persian) and the two of them were soon swapping words. By the time they had covered a few pages of Tony's ever-handy phrasebook, darkness had fallen and we were glad to accept the teacher's offer to spend the night in his school, where we should at least be able to tidy ourselves up for an entry into the capital the following morning.

We slept on the floor of what must have been the masters' common-room, a tiny whitewashed cell barely furnished with table, chair and a portrait of the Shah. Jolly scholars woke us up, pushing their shining morning faces through the window, and we washed at a pump in the yard in full view of their roll-call.

The schoolmaster brought us tea and bread and when we thanked him for his kindness he said gravely: 'It is my duty.' I was to hear this phrase again from teachers, who always went out of their way to be helpful, so that I wondered if some ministerial directive might have been given them telling them to be kind to foreigners, as though to redress the wave of xenophobia engendered at the time of the oil takeover.

Thirty welcome miles of new tarmac ribboned to Teheran. We were soon in the suburbs, past the airport, and past the Coca-Cola factory—a smart new building through whose wide glass front people were peering at the bottles that revolved in graceful balletic gyrations on an endless belt. This fascinating toy, I observed from a plate on the side of the machine, was a SYN-CRO-MIX Beverage Filler, made by the George Meyer Mfg. Co. of Cudahy, Wisconsin, USA.

Teheran sprawls over a flat plain that slopes upwards from its northern suburbs towards the Elburz, the great mountain chain shielding the southern shores of the Caspian. To the east, beyond the town, I caught a glimpse of Demavend, 18,600-foot sister of Ararat and Fujiyama. The *Daily Express* had announced that

Diana planned to be the first woman to gain its snowy summit, but we learned that a certain Mrs Summerscale—and probably other ladies besides—had made the ascent, and there seemed to be no point in making the long, but easy, hike where Mrs Summerscale had trod before.

I had heard rumours of a Hilton Hotel in Teheran. But it turned out not to have got beyond the planning stage. (Apropos the Istanbul Hilton a smart Persian girl said to me: 'I've heard from all my friends that it's very ostentatious and vulgar.'—I was pleased to point out that it was nothing of the sort.) We tried the Ritz (no relation), the Park (no room) and the Caravan (no dogs), and in all the prices were exceedingly high. In the end we slunk into a backstreet building with a name like Majestic or Continental, soon known to us as the Hotel Baudelaire. I am a connoisseur of small unstarred hotels and was immediately at home in the scruffy whitewashed room, with the brass bedstead and sagging springs, the voyeur's hole plugged with a matchstick, the crisp hair in the cracked basin, the attentive mosquito (anopheles?) on the rim of the crinkled lampshade, and its kind carelessly squashed in their own blood on the walls. But it was cheap and they were kind to Karrabas, who was now too big for his briefcase. The Baudelaire was not, however, cheap enough for Tony, who cast himself adrift and staggered off with his knapsack and broken bike to look for a suitable public square.

Teheran had all the aspects of a rapidly developing modern city, with wide boulevards full of enormous American cars with flashing fins and two-tone colours (*café and café-au-lait* seemed the most popular) driven at desperate speed by their death-defying Iranian owners. There were smart Mercedes buses and taxis of every breed (the Vauxhall 'Wyvern' was popular on account of its smash-resistant chassis, but since it has been re-modelled the demand has fallen off). Enormous government buildings were going up all over the place, great marbled monsters that dwarfed even the neo-Sassanian giants of the Reza Shah building wave.

Other manifestations of modernity were the new television station installed by RCA and privately financed by Iranians (transmissions had not yet started, but some thousands of sets had been sold in anticipation), and the new department store operated by Germans and reputedly backed by the Shah—a smart building with a lift (customers in *chadors* (veils) were forbidden to ride on it in case they got caught in the machinery), and well-stocked counters selling everything from detergents to dirndls. Modernity at its simplest level was represented by the penny-in-the-slot kerbside weighing machines personally supervised by their proprietors, on which unsophisticated ladies learned their weight probably for the first time in their lives.

From the hot centre of the town long tree-lined avenues led up towards the hills behind, bare and brown except for streaks of green where villages lay in watered clefts. On these slopes were the villas and swimming pools of the rich, and a perceptible drop in temperature could be felt in the short time it took to reach them. Here was the happy hunting ground of the real estate investors, with title deeds to plots changing hands and value daily like stocks and shares. Money was expensive. The rate of interest charged in the bazaar was as high as 20 per cent. 'If I had £50,000 I could be a millionaire!' said a Persian business man in the bar at the Park.

I called at the British Embassy to collect mail. It is hidden behind a high wall and enclosed in a large park, a valuable piece of real estate rivalled only by the next-door Soviet Embassy, which the Russians occupy rent free in exchange for providing the Iranians with a handsome Embassy building in Moscow. Both Embassies have equally large and leafy summer headquarters higher up the hill. The British go one further and maintain a week-end camp at the foot of Demavend for the summer relaxation of their employees. For all I know they may run a ski hut as well, for skiing is popular in winter.

The intervening streets between the British and Soviet Embassies are named Churchill and Stalin, in honour of the protagonists of the 1943 Teheran Declaration, by which the post-war integrity and independence of Iran was guaranteed by the powers who so summarily denied it for the duration. Roosevelt, the other member of the Teheran triumvirate, is commemorated by an avenue running up to the US Embassy on the edge of the town.

Victoria Regina proclaimed her power above the gate. Two smart Pakistanis in khaki uniform and blue caps stood on casual guard. Having collected letters from a pigeonhole in the porter's lodge I called on the Press Secretary, Dennis Spears, whose name I had been given in Ankara. He was 'in conference' and while waiting for him to emerge, I saw his deputy, a young man whose

The Black Sea looking
inhospitable

Sturgeon hooks

Military transport above the River Çoruh, Artvin

first post this probably was. As we talked, a breezy Iranian news-hawk blew in, who, amongst other things, was the Teheran corre-spondent of the *Daily Express*.

'Anything hot?' he asked. 'Nothing outside the handout!' replied the junior diplomat. At that moment a consignment of films was delivered. 'More propaganda, I suppose!' said the Iranian gaily rather than cynically.

Later I asked Spears what was the current Russian propaganda policy in Iran. At that moment it was one of 'sweetness and light,' he said. 'You know, women athletes, student exchanges, and all that sort of thing. They put in sixty-five hours a week broadcast-ing time, mostly directed at trying to break up the Baghdad Pact.'

Spears passed me on to Hugh Carless, First Secretary and Political Officer. I was keen to meet him as he had been *en poste* in Afghanistan and had lately travelled in company with a friend of mine called Eric Newby in search of some mountain in un-plumbed Nuristan.[1] Unfortunately Carless was in the midst of packing up to return to England (a servant entered with a recently labelled case of shotguns), and was too busy saying good-bye to his friends to have much time for me. He advised me against travelling via the northern route in Afghanistan with Diana and quoted the discouraging story of the American, Winant, who had been that way with a Swedish girl—the pair of them had never been seen again.

'Go and talk to John Bowling and see what he thinks,' Carless said. Bowling was a great friend and his opposite number at the US Embassy. The two of them had made several trips together into the interior of Afghanistan.

Outside the Embassy I ran into Tony. Poor Tony was very depressed because the spare parts for his bicycle had not arrived and he was rapidly running through all his money. He had teamed up with a kindred spirit, a young American called Tom, who also had plans to go to India the hard way, harder in fact, than Tony—on foot. (I detailed these examples of hardy travellers to a French diplomat and he trumped my ace by telling of a party of his compatriots, spastics, walking to India on crutches.) Tom had rich relations and showed me a postcard of a country scene in Virginia. It was from his brother-in-law and on the reverse I read: 'Martha

[1] For an account of this adventure see *A Short Walk in the Hindu Kush* by Eric Newby.

3

and me will be coming out to Afghanistan in the Fall. We're bringing the Cad. so who knows before long we shan't all be picnicking together on the banks of the Oxus . . .'

I rang up John Bowling at the American Embassy to ask him to lunch. He kindly returned the compliment by inviting us. The US Embassy is a large rectangular red-brick building, undistinguished but practical in appearance. It was completed in 1952 and, after the temporary lowering of the Union Jack in the British compound following the nationalization of oil, became one of the largest American foreign posts.

In the foyer a uniformed sergeant of marines, his name inscribed on a wooden plate on the desk, controlled the entrants. Bowling was called and met us in the passage, a short, smudge-moustached man with a walk somehow reminiscent of Groucho Marx. He took us down to lunch in the very functional canteen in the basement, where various Embassy employees sat eating standard American fare such as the hamburger. At the table next to ours a toothy fourteen-year-old girl was reading an obsessive comic called *Mad*. Sitting there eating hamburgers in the middle of Teheran I felt pretty schizophrenic myself.

John was a career diplomat. He spoke good Farsi and was busy learning French from a tape recorder. Like Hugh Carless he enjoyed seeing as much of the interior of the country as he could, and had made several trips into the Elburz with mules. He elaborated the story I had heard from Carless, telling how the young Winant, a relation of the former Ambassador to London, and a Swedish girl had been to India, where they had studied yoga and 'gone religious'. They were travelling north of Mazar-i-Sharif in Afghanistan, hitch-hiking and begging their way in the approved ascetic manner, when they had utterly vanished. Notes had been exchanged with the Russian government (it was thought that they might have crossed the frontier), but John was convinced that Soviet protestations of ignorance were genuine. I like to think they are still around—perhaps they crossed into Tibet via Wakhan. There was another awkward story of a party of Americans, including a woman, being murdered in 1957 in the eastern desert of Iran. When I suggested keeping Diana covered up under a veil he said,

'For God's sake don't do that or they'll think you are making off with one of their women!' This was a sound point.

John's house was a little way up the hill and he invited us there for a siesta. His shelves were well stocked with Science Fiction, though he claimed lately to have graduated to fact. His walls were decorated with framed photographs of sections of the heavens and he took us up on to the roof to look through his telescope, with which he was observing some obscure nebula for the Geophysical Year programme. There was a military barracks immediately across the road and according to John they thought that his sole reason for installing a telescope on his roof was to observe them. When I laughed, John said,

'That's nothing to what they say about you British. They seem to think you have a hand in everything. Why, an old man came to me once and complained that because he supported Mossadeq your government had caused his son to fail in his exams!'

John kindly invited us to make use of his basement rather than remain in the Hotel Baudelaire. I was planning a quick trip to the Caspian to look over the sturgeon fisheries, and as I should have to come back to Teheran to collect an urgent letter, I suggested we might stay the night on our return.

To further my sturgeon plan I was advised to call on the Ministry of Radio and Propaganda representing myself as a writer interested in reporting on the industry, as indeed I was. At the Press Office I was taken in hand by a merry middle-aged Persian gentleman called Moshiri. Mr Moshiri was working through a mound of clippings about Iran from British papers. I hoped it was a friendly batch because the Persians are notoriously sensitive to adverse comment: a Dutch journalist friend in London warned me that as long ago as 1954 he had recounted in an article a perfectly harmless Teheran joke about the Shah and had not been able to get a visa ever since. In 1937 a facetiously French journalist made play with the words Shah and *chat*. Moslems do not like being compared to animals and the Iranians had reacted by ordering all their government-supported students in France to return home.

But Mr Moshiri seemed in a mellow mood and we had an agreeable chat on a number of subjects. Mr Moshiri was planning to go to London again; after Rome and Nice it was his favourite city. He recalled the agreeable days he had spent there, the pleasant walks in Kensington Gardens, and the instructive hours in the Natural History Museum. He had stayed in an inexpensive boarding-house with a Persian friend of less sedate habits, who lost all his money at Brighton Races. When the landlady would not allow him to stay on without paying his rent he became very abusive about Britain and British landladies in particular, but Mr Moshiri had struck a blow in their defence by pointing out to his friend that perhaps their particular landlady had responsibilities towards the owner of the house, for whom she acted as manager.

Mr Moshiri interspersed this little narrative with dry chuckles and to my great delight he emitted that sound which writers transliterate 'Tee-hee' like Enid Blyton's gnomes. Robert Byron, whose travels through Persia are described in *The Road to Oxiana*, makes frequent use of this expletive, in which I had never really quite believed. But dear Mr Moshiri said it all the time—'Tee-hee'—I can hear him now!

Mr Moshiri was planning to send his son to a business college near Swansea, and I undertook to look after him when he passed through London. Somewhat in the spirit of the *quid pro quo* Mr Moshiri gave me an official introduction to the Governor of the *Shilat*, the fisheries at Pahlavi.

9

CAVIAR ON THE CASPIAN

ACROSS the Elburz lay the Caspian provinces of Gilan and Mazenderan, the country of the *Jangalis* or *Jungle Dwellers*, to me a land of mystery where the *maral* stag roared in the forests and the Hyrcanian tiger lurked in the boxwood thickets and strolled openly on the beach at night-time. It was in those regions that after the Great War a Bolshevik naval flotilla harried the retreating remnants of Denikin's White Russians, and with the help of a local 'bandit' called Kuchik Khan, established the Soviet Republic of Gilan, a forerunner of Azerbidjan and Kurdistan. It had survived until the signing of the Irano–Soviet Treaty of 1921 by which the Russians renounced their Caspian concessions while establishing their right to send forces into Iran if the country ever became a base for anti-Soviet activities.

This was the caviar coast, and our intermediate sortie would take us over the mountains to Chalus, thence along the coast to Pahlavi and back to Teheran via Khasvin. Armed with Mr Moshiri's letter of introduction and news of a British naval officer called Michael Gillam, who was said to be giving instruction in frogmanship to the Persian Navy, we gratefully quit the cauldron of Teheran and struck up into the cooling hills.

The Chalus route was said to be the prettiest: its passage up the southern slopes of the Elburz could not, however, claim to be anything but uncompromisingly austere. It was not until we crossed the watershed (via an 8,000-foot pass with the choice of a mile-long, leaking tunnel or a magnificent, but precipitous overland route impassable most of the year) that a more interesting geography lesson began.

Below the snow line was the tree line, straggly firs to begin with, thickening into leafy woods of evergreen—cypress, juniper and yew. The road curved steeply downwards giving sudden glimpses through rocky gorges of distant snowy peaks. We spent the night on a turfy promontory jutting out into the Chalus river. Its noisy downpour kept us awake all night, but we were compensated by the pleasure of a morning dip in a pool beneath an overhanging alder.

The early sun slanted through glades of oak. (Most of the barrel staves for British beer are made from the oak trees that grow in the Caspian forests.) As it became hotter the bitter smell of box began to fill the air and the road dived through cool green tunnels of hazel and pistachio. The river we had been following began to widen and spread into several streams; it was now entering the coastal plain and rice-fields took the place of forest. The rice was in the process of being planted: humped buffalo were ploughing up mud in the terraced pools and bending women with their legs akimbo and bottoms thrust out were speedily shoving wisps of green into the watery ground. This was an entirely Oriental scene and difficult to reconcile with what had passed immediately before.

We came down into the sub-tropical plain and felt the new humidity in the air. Rice-fields were all around us, still with wattle-protected patches of green seedlings not yet planted out, and watch platforms against the possible depredations of wild pig. Chalus had white buildings and lines of lemon trees down the middle of the road, and a seaside resort air with charabancs and little sidewalk shops that might have sold buckets and spades (but did not).

The Caspian was soon beside us. Though eighty-five feet below sea level this enormous inland lake looked much like the Adriatic on the Italian side, with an endless sandy beach lapped by a sluggish surge. In our enthusiasm to identify ourselves more closely with a new environment, and to avoid the terrible potholes in the road, we took to the beach and for some miles drove ecstatically along the strand, past concrete bungalows and plots marked out for future exploitation. A sea eagle with a fish in its beak flew low past us and I accelerated to pursue it. A shallow stream ran across the beach to the sea and before I could think twice about crossing we were in the middle and deeply embedded in soft sand. Water was awash over the floorboards and our belongings were afloat in the back. The car had been baptized in the Caspian with a vengeance and had it not been for two men who helped us with poles and planks, it would most likely have been buried there, for it was slowly sinking deeper into the sands. Soaked already we went for a swim still in our clothes, sampling the taste of its slightly salty water (it is three-eighths of the average ocean salinity). It was sandy and opaque and no good at all for goggling, so we lay on our backs looking up at the sunny snow-peaks of Elburz, which descended in the manner of a Chinese watercolour through ranges of misty forest over which black rain-clouds were poised like enormous parasols.

The cultivated verges of the now-regained road soon opened out into expanses of box and scrubby oak, with little houses intricately constructed of tree-trunks and clay and thatched with rice straw that often tapered into strange lop-sided shapes, the sort of houses inhabited by Grimm woodcutters or even, at worst, a witch. The women wore pyjama trousers, smocks coming down below their knees and shawls over long, black plaited hair. They would look you squarely in the face and seemed totally un-related to the shy veiled ladies on the other side of the range. These were the *jangali* people, inhabitants of the *jangal* or jungle.

Our agreeable sensation of visiting remote tribes and out of the way places was soon tempered by the sight of a collection of brightly painted buildings constructed in the angular architecture of early expressionism. A sign by the road said GHOOMOTEL, and though as yet uncompleted it would clearly be ready in time for the summer season.

Civilization was brought to these shores by Reza Shah, irascible six-foot-two father of the present Shah, who came into power in 1921 when a colonel in the Cossack Brigade stationed on the Caspian. Having attempted to oust the Soviet occupiers, Reza Khan, as he was then called, marched from his base at Khasvin (it is said at the suggestion of the British Legation) and established himself in power in Teheran. An Anglo–Persian Agreement, sponsored by Curzon, was signed, but the *Majlis* refused to ratify it, nor were its imperialistic implications popular in all sections of British opinion. Instead the Persians played one of their favourite tricks by immediately signing the 1921 Irano–Soviet Treaty.

Reza Khan was proclaimed Shah-in-Shah four years later and became to Iran what Atatürk had become for Turkey. 'Let there be tourism!' he seems to have said in respect of the Caspian coast, and lo and behold! gingerbread towns were laid out, and hotels were built and everything was laid on except the tourists.

Reza Shah's most notable contribution to tourism was the great hotel at Ramsar, where we stopped for lunch. It was beauti-fully placed on top of a hill, fronted by lush tropical gardens that swept down to the sea where a long white casino ended a splendid mile-long vista. The outside of the hotel was embellished with fantastic tinny statues of lions, fierce Sassanian warriors, and naked ladies holding aloft lamps, half-sisters to the nymphs who ring the Paris Opera. These lions and ladies, cast about thirty years ago in some royal foundry, are to be met with all over Iran in palaces and public places, a sort of trade mark of Reza's artistic patronage.

There were a number of people lunching in the large dining-room. American accents cut clearly through the chatter, emanating from executive-looking groups no doubt composed of technical advisers rather than tourists. I had heard rumours that sites for rocket emplacements were being reconnoitred, part of the Baghdad Pact ring from Turkey to Pakistan.

After an excellent meal served by efficient tail-coated waiters, we walked out into the garden. A heavy rainstorm, followed by fierce sun, brought out the sexy smell of orange blossom and damp, steamy earth. The air was debilitating, almost tangible, and very bad for the temper.

We drove inland along the widening coastal plain, through fertile fields of rice, tobacco, maize and tea. At Rasht, a town of wooden Russian-style buildings with red roofs, verandas and elaborately decorative metal gutters, we turned to the sea; fifteen miles along a straight road to the north lay Pahlavi, our immediate destination. Six fishermen, each carrying Tobias-like a large brown fish, asked for a lift and piled on to the car. Outside the town we were stopped at a control point and sailors in 'snow-drop' tin hats and white duck suits closely inspected our credentials. At first they would not let us pass, Pahlavi was 'off limits' for foreigners they said. But Mr Moshiri's letters did the trick. On presenting them we were allowed to continue but passports were retained against our return.

The town was not strictly Pahlavi, which lay across a lagoon to the east, but a suburb called Ghazian. In the little square we found a hotel called the 'Royal'. They had rooms and they knew 'Geelam', the British naval officer. The doorman set off to find him while we went inside to investigate.

It was an old hotel, built in the style of Czar Nicholas, with a rambling hall and passages and a courtyard with palms and creepers. We were removing our luggage from the car when a

jeep roared up containing two smart naval officers in white
uniform and a stocky, tousled figure in khaki shirt and shorts.
The latter was Lieutenant Michael Gillam, RN, and his companions were officers in the Royal Iranian Navy. He seemed
surprised and amused to see us, but there was no time then to
compare notes. 'I'm in one hell of a hurry!' he said. 'There's some
grim dinner in aid of a departing admiral at the hotel this evening,
and I've got to go and dress for it!' We arranged to meet after
the celebrations were over.

In the dining-room an L-shaped arrangement of tables occupied
most of the room. The great banquet was in progress as we
entered, and we caught Gillam's wink from behind a bowl of
flowers. We sat down at our little table beneath a picture representing 'The Cossack's Farewell' and surveyed the scene. All the
notables of Pahlavi—the mayor, the governor, the harbour
master, the chief of police, the departing admiral, the relieving
admiral, and various naval officers—were tucking into a chicken
stew. They were accompanied by their ladies, elegantly dressed in
almost (pre-sack) the latest fashion.

After dinner there were speeches; then the gathering broke up,
its component parts lingering self-consciously in the courtyard.
Michael Gillam detached himself towards our table and suggested we make up a party and go down to the night-club on
the beach. We piled a few naval officers into the car and drove
down to a gay bar with a gramophone and large stocks of drink.
It was called the 'Casino di Paradiso', but was known locally as
'Plage Mansur', after its owner. We were joined by the outgoing
admiral, for whom Gillam expressed great admiration, and
between us we drank several bottles of vodka, which is made in
large quantities in Iran and is the favoured drink of the not-too-
conscientious Moslem in the northern part of the country.

The following morning we met at the newly-built Diving
School, a concrete building on the beach, where Gillam proudly
showed us his equipment—the rubber suits, the flippers, the
oxygen cylinders, the pressure gauges—all of British pattern. His
appointment as Diving Instructor to the Persian Navy was something of an anomaly, for under the terms of the Irano–American
military agreement only the States are allowed to supply arms and
assistance. The American general, when he heard of the Royal
Navy's infiltration in the Caspian, is said to have protested and

3*

asked for Gillam's removal. But when he was told that the
Persians were in fact paying for the services they were receiving,
the matter had to be dropped.

Michael Gillam was thoroughly enjoying his job and had made
a very good name for himself in Pahlavi, though he sometimes
found it difficult to live down the regrettable lapse in British
naval tradition when in 1942 they sank the entire Persian Navy
sitting at anchor in the Gulf, when not in a state of war, and,
according to their version, the morning after the Persian officers
had been entertained to cocktails by a British oil company. A
large number of Persian sailors died in this very unfortunate
incident. I was able to point out in mitigation that the oil company had no knowledge of the Navy's plans and several of their
employees were killed in the subsequent landing of troops.

We went swimming with two Persian officers—a serious one
who had done a course at Portsmouth and a more flashy one who
had been trained, like most of the Iranian Navy, in Italy. The
latter was accompanied by his 'fiancée', recently imported from
Italy, a luscious blonde who boldly wore a bikini and was
nothing if not what our friend Brewster back at the Hilton would
have called 'well stacked'. A little way down the otherwise
deserted beach a small group of bathers were breasting the sullen
waves. Michael, who seemed to know everything about everybody, said that they were members of a Russian Purchasing
Mission, unsociable gentlemen who 'kept themselves to themselves'.

The nearby port of Pahlavi, visited that afternoon, showed
other Russian influences at work. An enormous dredger was
working in the harbour opposite the Shah's yacht and a few feet
away from British-built launches of the Iranian Navy. The
Hammer and Sickle was embossed on her funnel; life-belts named
her home port as BAKU. When I began to take a photograph a man
on the bridge sent for one of the crew who returned the compliment by photographing me.

The dredger must have had a full-time job to keep the port of
Pahlavi open. The level of the Caspian is said to be dropping at
the rate of eight inches a year and all the harbours are rapidly
becoming unusable. Weed marks on the piles below us made this
point apparent. Nobody quite knows why the Caspian is drying
up. Some people think that there is an enormous hole in the

middle, others ascribe it to the vast irrigation and power projects on the Volga. The Russians have for many years planned to raise the level by digging a canal to connect with the Black Sea.

Beyond Pahlavi there was a fine beach. Being *Jummah* it was crowded with picnicking families, among whom cars, buses, lorries and bicycles were speeding up and down, for here the main road took suddenly to the sands. This was the beach favoured by the citizens of Rasht, who, according to our Iranian friends, were notoriously 'rich, mean, stupid and cuckolds'. There are as many stories about *Rashti*, most of whom are Armenians, as there are about Aberdonians and we were given the following example that nicely combined their various characteristics: A rich merchant of Rasht caught a man fondling his wife's breasts. 'Stop!' he cried. 'You are interfering with the milk supply of my child. . . .'

We established ourselves under one of a long line of awnings, sitting on a carpet-covered platform with a supply of pickled sturgeon and vodka. A tall, quiet American came over and joined us. He was a timber expert from Oregon and was advising the Persian government on logging in the Caspian forests. He said that there were several other Americans in his team. They had landed up there having seen an advertisement in an Oregon paper offering 'A Challenging Job in Iran'. 'Some challenge!' he said. 'Would you believe it, the Iranians started clearing that stretch of beach down there to erect a timber mill? They wired off a great stretch of beach huts and started in with bulldozers. The citizens were kicking up one hell of a fuss as they didn't want their best beach all chewed up. That job would have gone ahead if I hadn't come along and pointed out the hazards of installing high-speed machinery on sand! A cutting mill on sand! Imagine!'

The Pahlavi *Shilat* is the largest of the five caviar processing centres along the Caspian coast of Iran. The establishment is surrounded by a high white wall which, in the days of Russian ownership, had formed a territorial enclave protected by armed guards. Under the new Iranian management there was a less restrictive atmosphere; they seemed to enjoy running their own show; there were no guards on the gate and the sun shone gaily on white buildings in the handsome colonial style of Czar Nicholas. Having sent up Mr Moshiri's letter of introduction I was shown into the director's comfortable office and over several cups of tea was treated to an outline history of the industry.

For some reason the sturgeon, unfortunate carriers of a sought-after commodity, prefer the Persian shores of the Caspian to those of its chief consumer, the Russians. But all parties, except the sturgeon, seemed satisfied when in 1893 an Armenian Russian living in Teheran called Stepan Lionosoff, obtained a twenty-seven-year concession giving him the fishing rights along the entire Caspian coast. (Ten years later an Australian named W. K. D'Arcy obtained an even more lucrative concession concerned with oil.) The Shah of the day was reconciled to the arrangement by the payment of money into his treasury and the fact that he could argue that in any case the fish was '*haram*', that is, forbidden to Moslems as unclean. Local gossip maintains that the Russians bribed a Mullah to express this judgement, which it is doubtful if Mahomet would have endorsed.

The Russians ran the fisheries with great efficiency and by the time of the Revolution they were employing several thousand people and had installed much valuable plant. All this was brought from Russia, sole market for the resulting product, not only caviar, but the flesh of the sturgeon and many other fish that filled this fertile sea.

In the first rapturous idealism of the revolution Trotsky, then People's Commissar for Foreign Affairs, undertook to evacuate all Russian troops from Persia and end the authority of the imperialistic Anglo–Russian Convention of 1907, whereby the two countries divided Persia into spheres of influence, the Russians claiming the north. Further notes included the renunciation of various Russian rights including the Caspian fisheries. These disinterested acts were subsequently qualified by a more realistic agreement which provided for the renewal of the concession, and despite the Russians withdrawing from the 'Soviet Republic of Gilan' they continued to occupy the port of Enzeli and operate the fisheries. The Iranian government was persuaded to give the monopoly to an official of the Soviet Department of Trade called Hassan-Kiadeh (after whom a Caspian fishing town is still named).

Meanwhile the heirs of Stepan Lionosoff, now on the other side of the fence, had protested that the cancellation of their concession was illegal. An Iranian arbitrating commission upheld their appeal and recommended that they be granted a further concession for fifteen years on condition that half the profits be paid to the Iranian government.

In 1924, perhaps regarding the Lionosoff interests as incompatable with socialist principles, the Russians proposed that the fisheries be leased to a company jointly owned by the two governments. To grease the wheels, the Soviet Government produced a sizeable cheque on account. But they had reckoned without the Administrator-General of the finances of Iran, a tough American called Millspaugh, who refused to receive the money into the treasury.

The Russians hit back at Millspaugh two years later when they placed an embargo on Iranian exports. Millspaugh resigned the following year and the fishery question was reopened with more success. In October 1927 a joint company was formed providing for an annual rental and a 50 per cent share in the profits. At the same time the port of Enzeli was handed back to its rightful owners and to celebrate this notable event was renamed Pahlavi in honour of Reza Shah, who had adopted this as his dynastic name.

The fisheries continued to be run by the Russians. Unfortunately the Iranian share of the profits under the 1927 agreement was non-existent owing to the fact that their co-directors, who controlled the sole market, could establish their own prices and run the company at a loss. This was a continual source of annoyance to the Iranians, who do not like to think that they are being financially victimized. In 1951, in much the same mood as Mossadeq nationalized the oil fields, they ended the Russian agreement, formed a government company, staffed it with Iranian nationals, and began to look for world markets. Today Russia imports only 38 per cent of the total production of Persian caviar (134.6 tons in 1956–57). The remainder goes to the USA (46.5 tons) and Europe (30 tons), leaving 6 tons for internal consumption, most of which is no doubt eaten in the embassies of Teheran.

After this history lesson, here supplemented slightly from other sources, I was taken on a tour of the establishment, which happily coincided with the arrival of a consignment of newly-caught fish being carried in by fishermen from a flat-bottom sailing boat on the creek.

The Caspian fishermen only rarely use the foul-hook method

favoured by the Turks. They rely on trawlers in the deep waters and long lines of gill nets offshore. My friend John Cauldwell, representative in Teheran of the famous British thread manufacturers J. & P. Coats, told me that he had tried to sell the Persians nets made by his firm but had been unable to compete with the Russians and the Japanese.

The fish were being carried in on wooden sleds. My gnomish guide pointed out that these were not the biggest sturgeon, the *beluga* or what he called 'elephant feesh', but 'middle feesh' and 'long nose' or sterlet. The *beluga* (*huso huso*) which averaged 150 lbs in weight and yielded up to 30 lbs of caviar, were mostly caught at the eastern end of the Caspian. The biggest *beluga* caught in Iranian waters weighed 850 kilos and was 42 metres long. My guide assured me—though it sounded like a fishing story—that one monster was taken out of the Caspian weighing 1,600 kilos which was over a hundred years old.

The newly-arrived fish, still forlornly waving their three fleshy whiskers and stirring feebly on their wooden biers, were carried into the operating theatre, a great concrete-floored hall, where they were well sluiced with water. Then, with a quick flick of the knife their bellies were slit open and a mass of glutinous black spilled into a metal container. The membranous matter still attached was separated in a colander-like utensil and the gleaming grey-black globules removed for further processing—mixing in borax for preservation and salt according to the consumers' taste.

That was not the end of the story as far as the fish were concerned. Those not sold for local consumption were taken to the large refrigerating chamber, which I entered after first putting on a padded coat and a Russian-style fur hat. A dim light shone in that frigid hall revealing ghostly carcasses, rigid as boards, stacked high on wooden racks. A frozen fishy smell stung my nostrils and the cold air penetrated my thin trousers so that I wished I had not refused the padded plus fours and leather boots worn by the workers.

There were other fish than sturgeon—stacked according to their breed—mullet, bream, carp, whitefish and catfish. The catfish looked enormous, with flat round noses and long whiskers. 'Are catfish nice to eat?' I asked my guide. 'Only Russies eat catfeesh!' he replied disdainfully. I was glad to quit that fishy catacomb and get back into the warm sun.

We next went to look at the laboratories where breeding and feeding research is carried out. Miniature long-snouted *sevruga*, looking like elongated sea-horses, were swimming round and round in long concrete tanks; larger ones, about a foot long, cruised more leisurely in a sun-protected pool outside. They disdained the shrimp-like sea-fleas I dropped before them. These fish, produced by artificial methods, will be thrown into the sea to produce their crop of caviar in due course. The Russians, apparently, had recently sent a paternal note to the Iranian government pointing out the dangers of overfishing.

Our final visit was to the packing rooms. Great wooden barrels of the stuff were lying all around, prior to being put into round tins for the markets of the world. White-coated tasters were sampling it with professional finesse and I was offered a plateful, not of the salty type I was used to (this is known as 'American taste'), but fresh-tasting. The globules, glutinous yet able to be separated with the tongue, popped against the roof of my mouth with a minute fishy plash. I must have eaten about £10's worth on the spot.

We travelled back to Teheran by the former Russian-operated toll road over the mountains behind Rasht. Beyond the watershed we came upon a scene of great activity with all the paraphernalia of destruction preliminary to some mighty work of construction. A large notice by the roadside read (one side in French the other in Persian) EMPIRE D'IRAN—OFFICE DU PLAN SEPTENNIAL—CONSTRUCTION BARRAGE SEFID-RUD. This was my first sight of an operation under the Seven-Year Plan, about which there had been a great deal of talk in Teheran.

The 'Plan Organization' was set up in 1949 to develop Persian industrialization. It was to be financed entirely out of oil revenues and consequently, during the period of the oil dispute when payments were suspended, it found itself very short of funds. With the establishment of the Oil Consortium a second Seven-Year Plan was provided for and now, under its auspices, major works were in progress all over the country.

In spite of opposition the administrators of the Plan decided to rely almost entirely on foreign consultants and engineers, the majority from the West, with the result that the country was full of Dutch, Danish, American, Belgian, British, German, Italian and French companies busy on the planning and construction of such important installations as steel foundries, sugar factories, fertilizer factories, power stations, cement factories, textile factories and dams. This particular project, the dam on the Sefid-Rud, was being undertaken by French contractors, Billiard, Compenon Bernard, and Hersent. A rugged pipe-smoking Frenchman, observing my interest in the elephantine scourings in the valley below, came over to the car and passed the time of day. He was one of the type of Frenchmen who work on great projects all over the world—the Congo, the Sahara, Indo–China. 'We are a special race,' he said, 'like your Scotch.' Then he used the phrase '*Nous roulons notre bosse*' which literally means 'we roll our hump', or 'we carry our house on our backs'. He pointed to the well-built little town on the hillside, complete with church, school, cinema and swimming pool. This was the *Cité des Cadres*, occupied by three hundred and fifty Frenchmen and their families, all enjoying a standard of living considerably higher than the local Iranians, who were still living in mud huts and earning 50 rials a day if they were lucky enough to get work on the project. The Iranians worked quite well, he said '*mais tout douce-ment*'. This dam, due to be completed in 1962, would cost 8 billion francs.

We soon began to wish that the Plan Organization had got busy on the road to Khasvin. We were continually, as was the custom of drivers in Persia whenever the road is bad, 'cursing the name of the John Mowlem Company'. Under the Plan this great British company was awarded one of the largest contracts for road con-struction (6,000 kilometres) ever given to a single firm. But there had been friction between them and the administrators of the Plan. It was held that their role was purely that of 'Consultant Engineers', with the actual work being farmed out to other firms and the equipment provided from various sources. But John Mowlem, so the Persians said, seemed to think they could do the job all by themselves, and without consulting anybody they had shipped in large quantities of their own heavy equipment. The Persians felt they were being told what to do in their own house and with a spate of unpleasant propaganda ordered the John Mowlem Company out of the country.

So bumpy was the road that at some stage one of our suitcases bounced out of the back (by the end of the journey almost every-

thing we originally set out with had disappeared in this manner).
We were lucky: a lorry driver pulled up at a tea house where we
had stopped and handed us the battered case saying that he had
picked it up thirty miles back in the road. As it contained all my
cash reserves, I was much relieved to see it.

Dropping down into the cauldron of Khasvin I noticed that
Diana, who had been silent for some time, was sitting with her
head between her hands. Her seat was far less comfortable than
mine, for apart from having to carry such frangible things as
cameras on her lap, she suffered from the hot air of the engine
which seared up through the loose gear-box cover near her feet.
It was always difficult to extract a complaint from her, but this
time I persisted:

'Are you all right?'

'Yes.'

'How all right?'

'Fairly all right.'

'Fairly not all right?'

'Yes.'

'Like death?'

'Yes.'

Then she began to cry and before I could console her she had
passed out. She was delirious when we got back to Teheran, where
mercifully there was John Bowling's house to go to and a bustling
Persian doctor from the British Embassy. She had some fever
which he could not put a name to, and for three days the poor
girl felt as if she was going to die.

During this period Karrabas caused me added anxiety by disappearing. I used to put him out in the cul-de-sac in front of the
house, and one day when I went to fetch him he was nowhere
to be seen. In the course of my door-to-door inquiries I came
upon a sly-eyed urchin who said that he had seen two men with
bicycles carrying the dog away.

I rushed off to look for them, asking every likely person if they
had seen anything. It became like a Kafka nightmare and every
Iranian face seemed to contain undertones of cruelty and vindic-
tiveness that could well have been concerned in the plot. After
several confrontations with the wrong dog I went to the police
station. 'You like dogs?' the hateful policeman said scornfully
after I had told my story.

Karrabas was away for two days and I kept it dark from Diana, who loved him. Then, on John's recommendation, I offered the urchin a reward of 100 rials if he could find the dog. He returned with Karrabas in ten minutes, perfectly happy but minus the tangerine silk handkerchief round his neck, I was uncertain whether to thank him or curse him.

As soon as her fever had subsided, Diana insisted on continuing the journey to Afghanistan, whereas by rights she should have recuperated for at least a week.

10

BABUL

Karrabas was growing fast and already developing characteristics of a reliable watchdog, giving incipient barks and making fiercesome rushes whenever strangers approached our camp at night. But the poor creature was not yet an accomplished traveller and on long hot drives he became fractious and unhappy. He liked to lie in the shade on the floor of the car where he was always getting in the way of the pedal controls, or else he would climb on to my lap and stick his head out of the canvas flap in the door to catch the breeze . . . Poor Karrabas! I began to feel that it might have been better to have left him with his brothers and sisters by the Black Sea.

He always barked in a certain way when he wanted to get out and go for a run. On the far side of the Elburz, crossed by another route that circled Demavend, I let him out beside a grassy field. Then a sad event occurred. Not realizing that the dog had crawled beneath the car to be in the shade, I ran the car backwards for a few feet. There was a slight bump and a terrible cry of pain and we urgently got out to find poor Karrabas moaning in the road. He was quite unable to move and whined piteously when I tried to pick him up. A great swelling appeared on his flank and I began to think that he had suffered some terrible internal injury. We got him into the car and managed to make him swallow some powdered aspirin in yoghourt. That night was one of the most uncomfortable I have ever spent. It was very cold and we had long ago lost most of our blankets out of the back. It began to rain and the place we had chosen to camp was covered in boulders. Karrabas needed continual attention and we took it in turns to nurse him through the night. But in the morning, though we were half dead, he appeared a little better. From his unsuccessful efforts to get up and walk it appeared that he was suffering from a broken leg and that the swelling, which had subsided, was a bruise caused by the pressure of his body against a stone on the road.

Outside a small town we found a hospital. We must have looked odd standing in the queue of very poor-looking people with

Diana clutching the 'unclean beast' to her breast, but the doctor, a young man with a pretty, pregnant wife who acted as his nurse, took our unusual consultation in good part, and diagnosed a 'broken arm'. Though unable to treat it himself he gave us a note to the vet at Babul, about fifty miles on.

Babul, down in the coastal plain, had some local importance as a cotton town. We were looking for somebody to direct us to the vet, when, as so often happened when we were in difficulties, a schoolmaster materialized and volunteered his help. ('It is my duty,' he said, when we thanked him.) The vet was in the act of inspecting the entrails of a baby chicken. He was a kindly, dedicated man and he soon had Karrabas lying on the wooden table and was examining him with professional aplomb. He thought the left foreleg was broken, and gave an injection to relieve the pain. Before he put the leg in a splint, however, he said I should take him to the big hospital for an X-ray. From this diagnosis it seemed we should be stuck in Babul for a time—not by the look of it, the most desirable place on earth. But the schoolmaster, who had been attending in the background brought some relief by saying surprisingly: 'There is an Englishman in Babul. Would you like to meet him?' Englishmen liked dogs and it occurred to me that we might leave Karrabas in his care and pick him up on the way back from Afghanistan.

The schoolmaster led us into a high-walled enclosure on the outskirts of the town. Beyond the courtyard were factory buildings with a high iron smokestack. A pretty Russian-style house stood in a garden of lemon and orange trees; beyond was a power house with a little balconied bungalow behind. From this humble building there emerged a short, wiry bow-legged figure in khaki shirt, shorts and plimsolls, who walked towards us with a questioning expression on his face.

The schoolmaster did the introductions. The name was Saunders and he was in charge of the power plant of the factory, which extracted oil from cotton seed. In the little bungalow we met his colleague, Schneider, an elderly Austrian who ran the extraction side of the business. Schneider was immediately sent off to get some beer.

'He'll be ages, so we might as well start on vodka!' said our host, as we sat down on his hard chairs and a bent old maid-servant brought glasses and a bottle.

Saunders talked with the non-stop rapidity of a man who has been deprived of congenial company for a very long time. We soon learned that he had been in Babul for almost a year, working for a local millionaire called Tehisatz, whose factory this was. He had a wife in England and a son, but he hadn't been home for twenty-four years, preferring to wander from contract to contract round the world, 'making good money and spending it', which, from his stories, he seemed to do almost in the tradition of the Canadian gold-diggers of the days of Robert W. Service. He had once worked for the legendary Williamson of the West African diamond mines at Alamasi, and went off into long stories about the fabulous 'booze-ups', when instead of just breaking gramophone records, they would destroy whole radiograms, which, according to his story, the millionaire mine-owner provided in quantity for this special purpose.

Saunders was fed up with Babul and though Mr Tehisatz wanted to extend his contract, he thought he would leave at the end of the year and perhaps take a job he had been offered in Pakistan. Nevertheless, he thought his employer was 'a fine old boy' in spite of the fact that they sometimes had tremendous rows. Mr Tehisatz would try and tell him what to do with the machines, whereupon Saunders would bring the generators to a standstill and the poor man would tear his hair and beg him to start them again.

'All right. Now we'll do it my way!' Saunders would finally say.

When he first arrived in Babul Saunders had lived in his employer's house, a handsome building across the road, but this had got so much on his nerves that he had asked to move into the bungalow. What really annoyed him was the fact that the Tehisatz children considered that they had right of access to all their lodger's possessions.

At last the old Austrian arrived with the beer. He was known locally as the *Khanum* or 'woman', because of his fussy ways. He was sixty-eight and had a pretty wife and daughter in Kitzbühel. Schneider complained bitterly that the local cotton produced such indifferent seed that it was impossible for him to do his job properly. Nevertheless the factory seemed to produce a fair quantity of cattle cake (exported to England), cotton, oil, *ghee* (used for cooking), and a rough-looking brown soap, long bars of which were stacked in a corner of the factory in very unattractive heaps. Pending the arrival from Hull of a 'Hydrogenation Plant', which was required for some process in the extraction of oil from the cotton seed, there would be no work for the *khanum* at Babul, so he was off to Teheran that afternoon for a week's holiday. He kindly invited us to make use of his room during his absence.

I took Karrabas to the hospital for his X-ray. A French-trained surgeon (the older generation of Persian doctors received their training in France, now Germany and America are favoured) laid him under the machine and photographed him from all sides. He did not protest, seeming to know that something was at last being done about his painful inability to get up and run around. I was to collect the photographs the following day and give them to the vet.

After lunch Saunders took us down to Babul-Sar, about fifteen miles away on the Caspian, a pleasant seaside resort with a good beach. There was a fine fisheries building and an old Customs house, but its former status as a port trading with Russia had lapsed and the harbour was badly silted up.

After a swim we went back to the hotel, a large establishment built under the same auspices as the one we had visited at Ramsar. While we were drinking vodka limes on the terrace, a big Cadillac drew up at the door. It had a royal crown on the number plate and I quite expected the Shah himself to alight, but it was only his brother's wife and some of her female friends. Chattering like birds and looking very Mediterranean in brightly-coloured shorts they disappeared inside. Apparently the pretty white palace across the road was not available to her, for she and her party were staying at the hotel. According to the Armenian manager of the hotel, an old friend of Saunders's, she was the daughter of M Ibrahim Zand, the Governor-General of Tabriz.

At the hotel we met the manager's son. He spoke English, having been educated at the American University in Beirut. He said that when we continued our journey we must not fail to call on his friend George, also an Armenian, who worked in Gorgan, on the road to Turkestan.

Saunders was anxious to show us all that Babul and its environs had to offer. In the evening we went for a tour of the town. In the course of our travels we called in at a little bar, which was also a toy and provision shop, and drank vodka and beer and ate pickled sturgeon in company with a number of schoolmasters who, like Saunders, were regular patrons. It was an outlet for Black Market caviar and I bought half a kilo for 150 rials. We drank a lot of vodka and I have a hazy recollection of being taken to the local cinema where we went up into the projection box to meet the operator, one of Saunders's cronies. He was apparently a Soviet citizen, and he wore a red star on his coat. The film was an Indian one. 'Hindi films always cobra!' a Persian maid-servant told me in Teheran, meaning that Indian films tended to have snakes in them as American films had gangsters; but this one was about elephants and maharajas and when it came to an end the Russian rapidly swivelled the projector to another aperture which served a second, out-of-doors cinema, and began the performance all over again. I could not ask him questions as he was so busy with his machine and in any case his English, according to Saunders, was limited to a few drinking toasts. So I was never able to establish if he was a refugee from Russia or merely a Soviet citizen working in Babul because they were unable to find a competent operator in Iran.

Karrabas made a lot of noise that night. So that he would be cooler and less disturbing to myself and others I put him outside on the balcony, where he lay quietly in a corner, glad of his change of position. Not long afterwards I heard a scuffle and a muted yelp. Thinking that the dog had perhaps fallen over the edge of the balcony I got up to investigate. As I came out of the door I saw a lean lupine shape slinking off fast into the darkness. Karrabas lay on his back with his head lolling sideways in a peculiar manner. I picked him up. He looked at me for a second and then he died. There was no blood on him. One of the factory watchdogs—a pack of three mean-looking alsatians— must have come upon the little interloper and resenting his presence in their territory had picked him up in his jaws and broken his back with a quick snap.

We buried him next morning under an orange tree in the garden. An old gardener dug his grave and some factory workers stood around as mourners. They thought we were quite mad. Alas poor Karrabas! I have told your story at such length to commemorate your brief life and to acknowledge my responsibility for its discomfort.

ALONG THE STEPPE

A WIDE coastal plain lay between the mountains and the sea. We found nothing to interest us in Sari, the provincial capital, and continued in an easterly direction. As we neared the southern corner of the Caspian, marked by the sitting port and railhead of the Teheran railway, Bandar-Shah, we passed a sweeping spur nicely spaced with cypresses and olives, which might well have been a corner of Tuscany even without the Italianate castello on the top. This was an intriguing building, the sort of place a millionaire might own near Monte Carlo. To inspect it more closely and in anticipation of an expansive view over the plain into Russia I followed the narrow road that curved up round the base of the hill. We were beneath the shadow of its crenellated walls when I saw a notice in English: 'ROYAL IRANIAN AIR FORCE. WIRELESS TELEGRAPHY TRAINING CENTRE. KEEP OUT'. There was an assortment of antennae sticking out all over the roof and I was speculating on their precise purpose, which I had a suspicion was other than that stated on the notice, when a jeep drew up alongside me and a voice said in English:

'No unauthorized persons allowed here. Are you authorized?' I said that I was not exactly authorized but had come to see the view. My questioner was a young and handsome man wearing an open shirt and a panama hat. He told us, perhaps a little brusquely, to follow him down the hill.

We soon regained the small town below. In the main street he stopped outside the largest building and ushered us inside. I imagined we were in for a police check and was resigning myself to an afternoon answering questions when I realized that we were in a hotel and that all he wanted to do was to offer us a drink. He ordered vodka and I fetched in from the car the remains of the caviar bought in Babul. Over the ensuing feast he told us that his name was Boris and that he was a Russian. That is to say, he explained, his father was Ukrainian married to an Armenian, who had left Russia at the beginning of the century. Boris had lived all his life in Iran, but the family still spoke Russian among themselves.

A Russian speaker! My mind jumped rapidly to speculation. Was he employed at the castle on the hill to eavesdrop Russian military wireless communications—fighter pilots to fighter pilots, tanks to tanks, in their Turkmenistan manœuvre areas? Was he keeping an ear on the Russian rocket ranges which were known to be a few hundred miles away over the flat steppe to the north? But whatever he was doing Boris was not saying and deflected my probings with professional finesse.

Boris had a Spanish wife and he wanted us to meet her. But we could not stay. He gave us his card with a message to his brother Peter, who lived in Gorgan. I then remembered that the Armenian George, to whom we had been given an introduction at Babul-Sar, also lived at Gorgan and I asked Boris if he knew him.

'He is my brother's best friend!' he replied. 'Peter will certainly be able to tell you where he is.'

Gorgan, formerly Astarabad, was no more than twenty miles on. We were arguing about the price of Coca-Cola in the main square when a local layabout came up and began the usual run of questions, this time in French, as to who we were, where were we going, why, when, and whence? It was difficult to remember that tourists were interesting phenomena in their own right: I was apt to assume that my questioners were members of the secret police and give them short answers accordingly. But whoever he was this young man earned his information by showing us where Boris's brother Peter lived. He had a workshop no more than a hundred yards down the road on the left.

The workshop was open to the street, a long low room filled with a conglomeration of machinery such as lathes and boring-tools, with irreparable pieces of engines displayed on the walls like trophies of the chase. Hard at work over a bench was a bull-like man with black hair, bright little eyes, and a black moustache. He looked up, coldly at first, but when I presented Boris's card, with the message written on the back, he stopped his work and came over to shake hands. He was very surprised to hear from his brother, whom he had not seen for several years and last heard of working in Teheran.

Peter spoke English with an enchanting accent and style which I find impossible to reproduce. He took us to his house next to the workshop and introduced us to his wife, telling us to stay there until he had finished off the urgent job he was then working on.

Peter's house had a pleasant little sitting-room in which (to us) the most important item of furniture was a large Frigidaire. From it his wife produced a great jug of a cherry-pink liquid, over which I made appreciative noises under the impression that it was some special local brew. She disillusioned me by producing a paper packet bearing the legend KOOLADE, and the *Good Housekeeping* 'Seal of Quality'. The next jug, soon in demand, was a deadly green.

Mrs Peter could speak no language known to me so there was a difficult silence until her husband returned with their five small children, who gravely shook hands and stated their names in piping trebles—Peter, Anya, Serge, Teddy and Valentine.

Peter asked me how old I thought his wife was. To be on the safe side I suggested thirty and was embarrassed when he said she was twenty-four. He had married her when she was fifteen. She was also of Russian origin and she had been his father's goddaughter.

Peter's father was by all accounts something of an autocrat. 'Everything must be done his way,' he said. 'If I put down my cigarette in one place, the old man orders me to put it some other place.' This was because he was ill, Peter explained. He had been to Philadelphia, at enormous expense, for some glandular operation and had been given a special medicine which miraculously kept him in better temper. But now the magic medicine had run out and the hospital in Philadelphia would not send him any more nor pass on information about the cure to Teheran, but insisted that he should return to Philadelphia if he wanted further treatment.

His father had started his workshop in 1903 and Peter said that it was the first to be opened in Persia. He had brought all the machinery from Russia. The father was at present in Teheran but would be back in a few days, and then all the trouble would start again. Peter wished he was working somewhere on his own like Boris, but he felt that he could not leave the old man alone. There were other reasons why he disliked Gorgan:

'It is no place for a woman here,' he said. 'I do not like her to go out into the street alone now. I had to fight a man with my fists the other day because he made an advance to her. This man took out a knife, but I was too strong for him. I think they are a little afraid of me here.'

It was late in the afternoon when we set off, accompanied by Peter, to find George. George, who had an agricultural advisory job under the Point 4 Organization,[1] was said to be working somewhere in the fields. We drove out of the town and along a rough road over the flat plain to the north, passing near clusters of *yurts*, the circular tents of the Turkomen tribes. It was dusk when we finally found him and a great red sun was spilling all over the western steppe. A combine was clattering cumbrously round a diminishing patch of wheat. Nearby a round figure with a solar topee pushed back on his brow was examining an ear of wheat. The whole composition looked just like a Soviet propaganda painting.

We drove over the stubble to meet him. Peter introduced us and we stood watching the Deering combine finish off its task. As the sun went down, little lights began to appear all over the steppe.

'Those are the combines. At this time of year they go on all night,' George said. 'Would you believe it, the Turkomen, who own most of the land round here, have bought over three hundred—combines, not tractors—this year alone!' I asked him if they got them from Russia and he said that the Russian type were too big and that the most popular makes were Massey-Harris and Deering.

We went back to the concrete building that served as George's office. He was concerned with improving the strain of wheat and specimen ears hung in bundles on the walls.

'The yield is not good at present as the land is very dry. But it will improve. Some of the American strains do very well here.'

George insisted that we return to his house in Gorgan and stay the night. He shared it with an officer in the Iranian Army, who was then away. But he had left his soldier-servant Ali behind and the willing Ali insisted that it was unwise to leave anything

---

[1] In his Inaugural Address, January 1949, Mr Truman defined the major courses of his policy. Point 4 in his list stated: 'We must embark on a bold new programme for making the benefits of our scientific advances and industrial progress available for the improvement of underdeveloped areas.'

A considerable number of American citizens were at large in the Middle East working on various projects known to the natives, at any rate in Iran, as 'Point 4'.

in the car. It was embarrassing to see our battered belongings, filthy blankets, spare tyres, petrol cans, and assorted rubbish carried delicately inside and laid out in the tidy hall.

George's mother was paying him a visit, a charming old lady, whom he was clearly very fond of. We sat down in the sitting-room and she brought a bottle of home-made wine, her special brew, very strong and acid. Then came dinner, yoghourt soup and fried meat, with a bottle of 'TK' sauce on the table, a local reproduction of such popular English concoctions as HP and OK.

We went to bed very soon after dinner. We were very tired and tomorrow would be Thursday, the day the Turkomen had their market at Pahlevi Diss, twenty miles out on the steppe. It was essential to arrive there very early, for by eight o'clock everyone would be going home before it became too hot.

I was afraid that we would be prevented from visiting this Turkoman Fair which various people had advised me to try to see. There had been no time the day before to get the necessary permit from the police and the station did not open until nine a.m. Hoping for the best we left George's house at about six a.m. but it was already hot by the time we were on the road leading to the north. A mean wind, laden with small grains of sand, whipped across the steppe into our faces. Two miles out of town we came to the police post, who remembered us from the evening before and allowed us to continue to Pahlevi Diss after we had left our passports and accepted one of their number as a passenger.

I expected the Turkoman market to be a colourful affair with all the goods of the Orient laid out—silverwork, fine saddles, silks and spices—and perhaps a display by fiery tribesmen riding mettlesome Arab steeds around the tents of some latter-day Tamerlane. But Pahlevi Diss turned out to be a seedy collection of stone buildings, with a solitary, dilapidated *droshky* standing in the potholed road. The market was taking place in a vacant lot at the edge of the town. The wind was now as hot as a hair-dryer, our eyes were watery and our mouths were filled with bitter grit. Through the hot haze I could see a straggly group of men and horses. It was a bitter disappointment: a closer look revealed several lines of goods laid out on the ground, their vendors squatting down beside them—cotton fabric, second-hand suits, salt, nuts, sweets, melons, blankets, and various shoddy products of the celluloid age. At least the men wore the right hats—fine shaggy sheepskin ones of varying dimensions, though not all could afford these and had to make do with little felt skull-caps. We wandered up and down the lines but did not see a single object worthy of purchase, with the exception of a second-hand shaggy hat, reeking of sheep, which Diana donned much to the amusement of the Turkomen, who hitherto had been unfriendly and suspicious.

We went to say good-bye to Peter back at Gorgan. I took the opportunity to get him to fix a new bolt to hold the engine to the chassis of the car. Two new bolts had already been fixed in Iran, but our progress had been so bumpy and the workmanship so bad that they had twice sheared off, leaving us to travel many miles with the great danger of the whole engine suddenly leaping out into the road. Peter went to work on his lathe—the oldest in Iran, he said, and pointed out its date 1902, and the name of its Russian manufacturer. Peter's bolt was so well-made that it survived the whole journey and even the appalling potholes of Afghanistan could not shake it out of place.

While Peter was working away on our bolt an old Turkoman, wearing a greasy Western suit and sheepskin hat, came in with a piece of tractor mechanism he wanted fixing. Peter asked him 600 rials for the job and the old man tightened his narrow eyes and with a shrug of the shoulders walked off down the street.

'He will come back, you will see!' Peter said. 'Nobody here can do the job as well as I can. Perhaps I will come down to 500 rials. But that old man is almost a millionaire.'

The United States Air Force 1:500,000 map which I was using marked an intriguing crenellated line running north of the Gorgan River for over two hundred miles across the Turkoman steppe to the Caspian Sea. It was named 'Alexander's Barrier', though apparently it was not built by or against Alexander at all, but, according to Dr Ghirshman of the French Archæological Mission in Teheran, by the Sassanian king Chosroes I (A.D. 531–79), to guard the 'front-door' of Iran against the incursions of the predatory nomads from Turan. It was known locally as the *Quizil Alang*, or Red Wall, and I was anxious to see what could justify such a positive marking on the map.

A road ran out into the steppe from Gorgan as far as Gunbad-i-Quabus, a seedy village named after the major monument that stands in its centre. This monument, built in the eleventh century to house the remains of a local prince called Shams al-Maali Quabus, reared distantly across the plain like a municipal water tower. Closer inspection did little to alter this impression. Built on a small mound its austere outline of brick, relieved only by ten buttresses and two thin bands of Kufic script, the 170-foot tower was capped by a conical roof scarred, so they say, by the shells of trigger-happy Russian artillerymen. I had hoped to use it for a view over the steppes, but there were no stairs inside, only a hollow shaft, for Quabus, who did not wish to be disturbed in his sleep, ordered that his body should be enclosed in a glass coffin and suspended by chains from the dome.

The Gorgan River ran beyond the village. A sentry guarded the old bridge and said that we could go no further. But I told him that I only wanted to see the *Quizil Alang* and should be back within an hour. He went into his hut without making it clear what he wanted us to do and by the time he had emerged we were across the bridge and heading in the direction of Russia no more than fifteen miles away at this point.

The ground was flat as far as the eye could see. Herds of camels grazed on desiccated stubble. Avoiding the black Turkomen tents, where we could not be sure of a welcome, we bounced on northwards. After several miles we came to a mound. Driving the car to the top we looked out and saw the line of earthworks stretching towards the Caspian. Time and weather had worn the ramparts, ditches and entrenched camps almost to nothing. But the line was still clearly visible and it must have looked even more like a landmark to American pilots who might happen to fly that way.

The sentry did not protest, so relieved must he have been to see us, when we returned across the bridge. After being beaten in a race across the plain with a young Turkoman driving a German jeep, we headed southwards towards the eastern offshoot of the Eburz.

It was an enormous relief to feel the drop in temperature as we climbed into the hills. As evening came we found ourselves in an entirely different world of old oak trees, ash and hazel, haunts of leopard, wild boar, and the *maral* deer. There were grassy clearings, with the lowering sun slanting through the trees, and rocky coombs with blackberries, clinging moss and ferns. The streams had trout in them and we swam in a shady pool. We passed a sign bearing the Shah's cipher. Nearby, invisible in the trees, was a royal hunting lodge, much favoured by his brother. We were now in Gulistan.

Peter had told me stories of robbers and tigers in these hills. Some friends of his had lately been waylaid and all their luggage had been stolen. And a local boy reported seeing a tiger only a few weeks back. Moved by these doubtless apocryphal tales, I set a circle of petrol cans around our camp that night to give some advance warning against intruders. But only the wind in the trees disturbed us, and the running water of a nearby stream.

These lovely forests ended all too soon and gave way to a wide and arid valley. By the time we reached Bujnurd some hours later we were hot and thirsty: the Coca-Cola trail had fizzled out fifty miles back in a muddy hole dug in the side of an irrigation ditch, where a boy had buried a few bottles to keep them cool.

We were filling up with petrol from a dump of five-gallon tins in a backyard, when a local youth, a pock-marked lad with a shifty eye, suggested by signs that we might like to go for a swim. There was a beautiful pool a few yards up that track there, he seemed to say, as he jumped aboard and insisted on guiding us there.

The almost palpable smell of a putrefying donkey followed us like a sickly cloud. After we had driven for several miles down a dusty track, I began to get impatient and urged him to find the pool quickly on pain of our disapproval. Then suddenly we came upon it, an oasis in the waste, and all was forgiven. Shaded by leafy plane trees, the pool was surrounded on three sides by bare and burning rocks. It was fed by a spring that gushed in beside a pretty domed building tiled in blue and yellow. On the hill above a larger mosque, similarily tiled, was undergoing repairs. It was an agreeable scene and had it not been for the buses and the large number of people congregating there, would have been idyllic. But it was Friday, and people seemed to have come from far and wide to spend their day of rest at what was probably the only cool spot for miles. It was called the Pool of the Five Brothers.

We immediately became the centre of attention and it was difficult to organize ourselves to take a dip. Mixed bathing was taboo and Diana was led away by a henna-haired harridan to a cranny in the rocks. The pool was full of small boys and large carp. I dived in the cool water and swam merrily amongst them. Diana was made to bathe naked in a little grotto by the mosque, the old women screening her with their black *chadors* held up like bat wings. Excitedly discussing her proportions, the old hags prodded and pinched and ducked her in the thigh-deep water, shooing away the crowd as if she were their private property.

After my swim I climbed the hill to take an aerial photograph of the pool. From this point of vantage, I saw a group of soldiers running in extended order round the base. It soon afterwards appeared that their manœuvre was designed to surround us, for when I climbed down again they were standing around the car with an air of a successfully completed operation. A young officer asked in English to see my papers, and when I replied light-heartedly that I did not see what business it was of his, a steely look came into his eye that caused me quickly to hand them over. He then said that the man who had brought us to the pool was a thief. This came as something of a shock for I had entrusted my wallet to his care while I swam. He had handed it back to me, but I had not looked at the contents. As a matter of fact nothing seemed to be missing from it. I gathered from the officer that the man was not a convicted thief but merely suspected of being a thief. Whether he and his men had come all the way there just to warn me against a putative thief, never became quite clear. The fact that we were at large less than fifty miles from the Russian frontier may have had something to do with their activity.

le style moderne:
Hotel Metropole, Tabriz

*assanian Baroque: Reza
hah's hotel at Ramsar*

Sturgeon fishermen arrive at the Shilat

Outside the cold storage room

12

MESHED

THE MAIN industry of Meshed is its mosque, a blue-domed gold-pinnacled wonder that houses the shrine of Imam Reza. Imam Reza was a close descendant of Ali, Mohamet's son-in-law, whom most Iranians, being Shi'ites, worship with a devotion that seems to be greater than is accorded to the Prophet himself, thereby cunningly dissociating themselves from their Arab conquerors who imposed His word upon them with the sword. Meshed is the premier place of pilgrimage in Iran and every year about half a million people visit the shrine and earn the right to call themselves *Meshedi*.

At first Meshed looked like living up to its reputation as a city of fanatics. Driving in down a long leafy avenue we saw a man lying in the road apparently dead. Nobody seemed to be making any effort to move him so we assumed he had gone off into a religious trance. Perhaps he was simply trying to die for 'to die in Meshed is to die holy'. Shortly afterwards we saw another man lying on the pavement, under the feet of the passers-by, with no clothes on at all. He was curled up like an embryo, a bony spine protruding above an emaciated bottom. He could not have been dead, for when I turned the car round to get a closer look he had vanished. These two occurrences, which may have had a perfectly simple explanation, put us a little in fear of the place, and temporarily discouraged Diana from her project to visit the mosque, which was strictly forbidden to Unbelievers.

Finding no room at the Pars, traditional hotel of the traveller, we cast desperately around for another, several times circling the large soapstone statue of Shah Reza and the mile-square precincts of the splendid mosque. We finally found a new hotel called the Ferdousi, which I am happy to recommend for its cleanliness and comfort. There was hot and cold water in the bedrooms and at the touch of a bell iced Coca-Cola could be materialized. In a showcase in the passage turquoises were stuck on to paper in the form of a necklace. They were windblown and therefore very cheap, but more expensive ones were also obtainable, according to the paper, from Akbar Ossoukian, 'concessionaire' of the turquoise mines at Nishapur, about fifty miles away. The Hotel Ferdousi, I learned, was owned by Akbar's brother.

Inevitably I paid a call on the former British Consulate, a favourite subject with travel writers since it was closed down following riots in 1952. The large white classical-style mansion, built in the heyday of Lord Curzon's concept of imperial control of a corridor from England to India, has become for them a symbol of the downfall and decay of the British Raj.

It was still a fine building, even if the effect was of a crumbling plantation house in the southern states of America. The plaster and the paintwork were peeling, the leafy garden was going to seed, and there was the sweet smell of dry rot in the spacious halls where great receptions were held in the days when, to use the words of Lord Curzon, officials were housed 'in a fitting way to represent to the native mind the presence of a great and wealthy power'.

But there was Mr Raj, the Pakistani caretaker, and he entertained us as graciously as any pro-consular hostess, serving us tea and macaroons in his saloon. After tea he produced a pile of photographs illustrating a recent grand occasion when the British Ambassador at Teheran, Sir Roger Stevens, had paid a visit to the former consulate. Mr Raj had organized a big reception, inviting all the Meshed notables in the name of Her Majesty the Queen. There they all were in black and white—there was Sir Roger, with his angular face, his unruly hair and his bony, intellectual brow, shaking hands with little Mr Raj; and there was the Afghan Consul; and there was the Chief of Police of Meshed and the Military Commander; that smooth-looking figure in the background was the Counsellor, Mr John Russell; and that square-jawed gentleman was from the Ministry of Works who had come all the way from London to consider the cost of repairs and the possible conversion of the Consulate into a base for the British Council. . . . It had been a successful, almost a shining occasion, and Sir Roger had written Mr Raj a charming letter of appreciation.

The American Consulate, the 'Konsulgari Amrica', was by contrast very much a going concern. Though less impressive externally and tucked away in a maze of back streets, it was a more agreeable building and had in fact been the private house of a rich Meshedi merchant who at the beginning of the century had made his money trading with Russia through Tashkent and Samarkand. It was built in the Russian style and still contained some of the original furniture—porcelain stoves, and Imperial-looking gilt pieces covered in crowns and eagles. Most of the furniture, however, was attractive American colonial.

The passage to the Consul's office was lined with Currier and Ives prints. I found him sitting under the Stars and Stripes. He was a young man, very friendly and hospitable, in spite of the fact that I could produce no very good reason for calling on him, unless to ask him about the American-operated radar station, slowly swivelling towards Russia, in the hills behind the town. But I felt it would be a breach of protocol to press this question, especially when he so kindly invited us to swim in the pool he had recently built in the garden.

The Consulate garden might have been a corner of England, with a green lawn and hollyhocks, roses and other traditional flowers. There was quite a party round the pool: the Consul, his wife and children, several Americans connected with Point 4, a tall Persian who I was informed was a *sayyed* or descendant of Mahomet (the 24th in line, no less), and his wife, a beautiful slant-eyed girl who they said was a princess and a descendant of Genghiz Khan. These last two should produce some interesting children.

I admit that a psychological allergy to Islam oppressed me in Meshed and I was glad to be on the move again. The last lap to Afghanistan was ahead of us and we might just have made it in a day had it not been for an unexpected interlude about half-way there.

A large piece of ironwork attached to the radiator came adrift and got caught up in the fan belt. It was an object that seemed to serve no useful purpose, but its present position made forward movement impossible. I was struggling in the midday sun to remove this appendix with our only remaining tool, a hammer, when a young man appeared as if from nowhere—it was a well-scoured sandy plain—and with the help of a piece of wire managed an effective repair. In return for his services we gave him a lift to his village, a few miles down the road. He invited us to his house for a siesta, insisting that nobody in their right mind travelled at that time of day. Gratefully accepting his offer we turned off the road towards an unpromising collection of mud huts such as I had often noticed along the way and pitied their occupants for the apparent poverty of their existence.

But when we were actually among the houses, in mud-walled narrow streets, they began to take on individuality and even charm, though a little whitewash would have done much to brighten things up.

Our friend led us through a gate in a wall, across a dried-up courtyard, and into a domed mud house. The main room, from which the women of the house were excluded during our visit, was carpeted with bright rugs and covered with cushions embroidered with simple flowers. Soraya and the Shah looked down from the walls among large photographs of spike-moustached relations of our host. The village gendarme now appeared and I thought that his visit was official until it was explained that he was the brother of our friend and had an equal share in the house. Tea was brought in a large samovar and we lolled back among the cushions glad that the mud roof provided such excellent protection from the sun.

Conversation was difficult as the young man spoke only a few words of English. First we were shown their joint collection of pin-up photographs, mostly ladies with bare tummies; then we compared notes about our respective families. The gendarme—he was in charge of the post, with six men under him—announced proudly that he had been married four times and was the father of seven boys. The brother, who was only seventeen and still a student at Meshed University, claimed one wife, married when she was thirteen, and two sons. In order not to appear totally insignificant in their eyes I made a compromise claim to two wives and four sons.

The talk then turned to hunting, or *shikar* as it was known in those parts. Would we like to come with him on a *shikar*? The young man produced a rifle (a .22) and pointed up towards the distant hills. What did they shoot? I asked. He did not know the word in English and drew a picture of an animal that looked like a dog. Seeing my bewilderment he added a pair of tusks. Was it a wild boar?—I made as if to eat and said 'Haram?' (unclean) and he nodded assent. Then he drew another picture more easily identifiable—a dog with curly horns coming out of its ears. I had expected this—it was some kind of mountain sheep.

The *shikar*, apparently, took place at night. First, while the sun was still up, we were to go for a swim in a river he knew. We bumped off across the dry earth and about three miles from the village came upon it. It was shallow and full of toe-tickling crabs, but it was cool and we lay happily in the water watching the eagles circling overhead in lazy spirals.

Beyond the river valley I had noticed what looked like the ruins of an old castle and I suggested to our friend that we should investigate it more closely. Following his directions I drove along the edge of the river in a muddy cart-track. The track then followed the bed of the stream, which had narrowed at this point, and was running fairly fast. Considering what we had already been through elsewhere this stream did not seem to be a very difficult proposition, and at least was better going than the mud beside it. But our wheels were soon churning up the gravel on the bottom and even the sacrifice of Diana's fur coat and a blanket under the wheels could not get us out. We were ignominiously stuck once again.

An old man was working in a nearby melon patch. We borrowed his long-handled spade and tried digging. But the current neutralized our efforts, carrying more pebbles into the holes we cleared.

'I will get my tractor,' said our friend. It had not occurred to me that he could be so grand as to own a tractor. He was either a local landlord or did not understand the use of possessive pronouns. He certainly seemed to have a seigneurial air about him, for commandeering the old man's horse he rode off confidently towards the village.

We sat sadly on the hillside watching the eagles in the sky and the orange-frilled woodlice on the ground until the sun went down. A wicked little boy on a donkey, looking like some eighteenth-century lady's depraved slave, rode over and watched us knowingly. The old man was worried about his horse and kept climbing the ridge to search the horizon. We were developing a sense of fatalism and not bothering too much about anything.

The young man did not return for about two hours. There was no tractor because it had gone to work in another village. Then an old jeep arrived, with at least ten people aboard and bristling with rifles. This was the *shikar* party: young bloods from the village accompanied, surprisingly, by a pretty young girl who peeped over her veil in a very provocative manner.

The jeep made several efforts to pull us out but in spite of the weight it carried it could not get a grip in the mud. There was nothing for it but to return to the village and await the tractor the following morning.

'Tomorrow night we go shikar,' said our friend consolingly as we walked sadly back and the rival band of hunters drove noisily off into the hills.

Back at the house the gendarme had been joined by a cousin and we all sat round the samovar and drank tea. No woman appeared, though I could hear female voices in the next door room. Two little boys came in to play, to be treated with great indulgence by their father, the gendarme. Then the visitor, for no apparent reason and without any preliminary announcement, got down on his knees and began to pray, throwing his head back and forwards on to a small disc of clay he laid on the ground (which explained the function of a similar object, stamped with the outline of a hand, I had picked up in the hotel bedroom at Meshed), waving his arms about and reciting his prayers in a rich sing-song voice of which he was obviously very proud. The gendarme looked askance at this exhibition and continued talking in a loud voice looking at us as if to say, 'Don't take any notice of him! He's only trying to impress upon you what a holy person he is!' When his private service came to an end the visitor joined in the conversation as if nothing had happened. Then came a supper of fried eggs swimming in grease and more tea from the inexhaustible samovar. Then the mattresses were made ready and we went to sleep.

The car rescue operation began early. As we set out on the tractor we met the returning hunters. Two mountain sheep were strapped to the bonnet of the jeep. They were female urial and lacked the splendid curving horns of the male. I think one of them was pregnant. From the hunters' description I gathered that their method was to hide up by the animals' drinking pools, switch on the headlights when they came to drink and shoot them as they stood dazzled by the beam.

The tractor succeeded where the jeep had failed. Back at the village the gendarme told me he had received a telegram. According to this message, 'Iskandar was not to go on *shikar*'.

(Everybody called me Iskandar, the Persian name of Alexander the Great.) Frankly, now that he knew how it was done, Iskandar did not want to go on *shikar* any more.

I was not able to establish the source of this injunction. Perhaps the gendarme felt he could not be responsible for allowing an Englishman to go wandering around in the mountains only a few miles from the Russian frontier and had concocted an imaginary message to save him from appearing inhospitable. Or perhaps he really had consulted some higher authority and had now received their answer.

The whole village turned out to see us off. The young man, who had developed a fervent admiration for Diana, looked actually miserable to see her go. I gave him a cheap compass as a consolation prize and the gendarme a large piece of pink soap for one of his invisible wives.

The Persian Customs operated at an unprepossessing little town a few miles from the frontier. After a terrible streetside lunch of mashed meat fried in long fingers and a lethal salad of mint and watercress we made for the Customs buildings. I should here like to offer a word of advice to travellers along this route—do not, unless you have all the time in the world, take no for an answer. It is the duty of the Customs in most countries to consider the interests of the traveller: it is a widely accepted principle in the East that the traveller must await the pleasure—be it dinner, siesta, family business, laziness or just plain bloody-mindedness—of the Customs. If I had accepted this point of view I should have remained in that stinking spot for at least another three hours. It is sometimes necessary to pursue vigorously the officials concerned, even to the extent of personally pulling them from their beds. They may mutter something like 'mad dogs . . .' but results can be produced if you make the effort.

On this occasion the galvanized Customs nearly had the last laugh. Such was my urgency (I hoped to reach Herat that night) that I did not tie up the door of the car properly and somewhere in the desolate three-mile stretch of no-man's-land between the two countries our passports slipped out on to the road. We quartered every inch of that burning section and failed to find them.

It was a situation that contained the seeds of desperation—if the passports could not be found we should in theory be doomed to spend the rest of our lives in zeroland, for neither Persians nor Afghans would let us through without them. Our only neighbour would have been an aged road-mender who was shovelling stones into potholes with sisyphean resignation. I then noticed that the dust from his labours was blowing horizontally across our path, indicating the existence of a fairly strong cross wind. It was just possible that they had blown into the ditch at the side. There, after an hour of searching, we found them. And the relief was exquisite.

I did not complain at the delay when we came to enter Afghanistan.

13

HERAT

It was night and a raddled moon cast leprous spots over the desert landscape. We were filled with an infantile excitement that now we were penetrating remote and possibly hostile country, that at any moment we might run into a band of those robbers so many people had warned us against. 'If they stop you,' I had been cautioned, 'on no account produce a gun. They will have you covered and it will give them an excuse to shoot first.' But in spite of this counsel I admit that I took out the Luger from the toolbox and fingered it thoughtfully, with echoes of Sir Henry Newbolt running through my mind . . . 'Ye have robbed, said he, ye have slaughtered and made an end . . .' 'He flung his empty revolver down the slope. . . .'

We drove across the ghostly old arched bridge across the Hari Rud and up on to a sandy, scrubby plain. The towering mud walls of a battered *caravanserai* gloomed down on the right. Diana clutched me nervously when a white figure stepped out from the shadows and stood in the middle of the road. Had we indeed fallen among thieves? Should I drive on and risk a bullet or should I parley with them and persuade them I had nothing of value? I fixed on a bronze knuckle-duster, parting present from a friend, and brought the car to a stop.

He was a wild-looking man indeed, waving his arms and jumping up and down like a banshee. But of course our fears were absurd: he was only a poor Afghan who wanted a lift to Herat. I made him sit on the mudguard, where we had rigged a comfortable seat for casual travellers, and as we speeded on I was surprised to see an endless ectoplasmic stream pouring out of his head towards Persia. It was his white turban that had come undone. With elaborate dexterity he rewound its enormous length only to have the same thing happen again and again. We passed a number of other people walking that lonely road. The cool of night seemed to be the accepted time for crossing that inhospitable stretch of sand.

We entered Herat shortly after midnight, having dropped our

grateful passenger on the outskirts and declined an invitation to stay the night in his house. The recommended hotel in Herat is called the Park; a lunatic boy on a bicycle undertook to lead us there and we followed his wobbling progress down long avenues of pine trees until he sat down happily by the roadside and refused to budge. Deprived of a guide it was some time before we found a notice, 'PARK OTEL', at the entrance to a large building set back in a grove of pine trees. They were evidently expecting us, for even at this late hour the staff (two men and a boy) were out on the porch in their pyjamas waiting to receive us, presumably warned of our approach by the frontier.

The ante-rooms were unexpectedly large, with tubular steel armchairs spaced around the walls, and a grand piano, and a showcase on the wall filled with all the luxuries of the West— packets of jelly, a bottle of chutney, sardines, a tin of lemonade powder. The beds were blissfully comfortable after the hard surfaces we had suffered for so long. There was a splendid shower, a favourite promenade for black beetles, but this was their hour and we could not complain. The lavatory was a rare specimen, a 'Little Niagara' by Shanks, but Niagara's water would not fall during our stay.

Our fellow guests, encountered the following morning, were a young Austrian called Max Klimburg, and his Afghan associate, Mohamet Ali. Max was a representative of a Viennese organization making what he called 'small farming implements'. Max was trying to persuade the Afghan farmers to use the scythes manufactured by his firm rather than sickles or the scythes they were in the habit of making out of motor springs. He explained that to be effective a scythe should be made of soft steel, whereas motor springs, being tempered hard, were quite unsuitable for the job. Mohamet Ali worked at the Afghan Ministry of Agriculture and though he had been trained in advanced mechanical engineering for the past year, had been reluctantly accompanying Max round the country trying to sell scythes. Mohamet Ali sadly explained that the Afghan husbandmen either preferred the time-honoured and relaxing method of sitting on their haunches with a sickle, or expected, in the name of progress and foreign aid, to be presented at least with a combine apiece.

It was pleasant to sit in the sun outside the hotel. Under the pines it might have been Le Touquet. Drinking tea by the goldfish pool we were joined by a tall young Afghan who asked in excellent English if there was anything we wanted. Diana said there was only one thing in the world she wanted and that was a Pepsi-Cola. She meant it as a joke, for this was a place where we estimated, even hoped, that it would not be obtainable. The young man gallantly replied that there was one bottle in the whole of Herat: it was his and it should be hers. He returned in a short time with the familiar brown bottle and we drank it warm and fizzy on the spot. The charming cavalier turned out to be the son of the Governor-General of the province.

There were various things to be done connected with the next lap of our journey. I planned to travel to Kabul, which we now learned to pronounce in the correct manner 'Carble', by the orthodox southern road through Kandahar, and return by the more rigorous route round the north armed with the necessary permits from the capital. The distance via Kandahar was about eight hundred miles and I was told by Amanullah, the English-speaking secretary of the hotel administration, that I should have to put in a written application for petrol coupons.

Herat was like a town plan without a town. I suspect it was conceived on Garden City lines sometime in the 1930s. This is not to suggest that Herat was not in existence before that, indeed it dates from before the time of Alexander the Great who used it as an advance base for his invasion of India, but it must have been about then that the main layout was put in hand. A system of divided roads, almost as wide as *autobahns*, radiated from the centre to disappear through the pinewoods into the desert beyond. There were a few large houses set back from the roads and at the frequent intersections circular concrete strongpoints guarded the policemen on point duty against being run down by donkeys, flocks of goats and the brightly decorated jaunting carts called *gaudis* that did the job of taxis. When the occasional car came along they made the most of it with fierce whistlings and urgent hand signals.

'BE CAREFULLY' warned a notice where the road led into the spacious rectangular city square. The fountain in the centre was embellished by a group of stone horses leaping weakly from the edge, inspired by the Roman splendours of Bernini but wholly lacking their nobility and scale. Depressed lamp standards strung with sagging wires surrounded a floral garden whose municipal blooms put up a brave show in the wilting heat. Beyond the square and the crumbling bazaar the five minarets of the *Musallah* stuck up like factory chimneys.

The petrol office was reached by climbing a wooden ladder from a pleasant shady courtyard. Within was a babel of turbaned lorry drivers excitedly pleading their cause for more petrol with the impassive arbiters behind the counter. As a foreigner I was politely given priority over the mob and coupons were filled in laboriously and passed to a succession of officials for additional signatures. Each coupon specified the name of the place from which the petrol was to be drawn; this as far as I was concerned, precluded the possibility of wandering too far in any unauthorized direction.

I drew my Herat ration immediately, locating the pump near the hotel, an early model with a hand lever and two glass containers that alternately filled with a brown liquid the precise colour of Coca-Cola. The smell of that petrol haunts me now, an evil, nauseating stench that seemed to contain something of the actual smell of death. This petrol, like all Afghan petrol at the time, was imported from Russia, though there were rumours that the recent *rapprochement* with Pakistan would permit them once again to import the Burma Shell products they had enjoyed before they had angered the Pakistanis with their embarrassing championship of an independent 'Pashtunistan', or 'country of the Pathans'. As this hypothetical state would have taken in a large part of north-west Pakistan the Pakistanis had felt compelled to express their disapproval with a few economic sanctions.

But the Russian petrol was cheap enough—under two shillings a gallon. This compared favourably with Turkey and Persia—it was only in tax-happy Europe that it rose to as much as six shillings a gallon. The Russians, like a number of other countries, call their petrol 'benzin', but the Afghan is still faithful to the Anglo-Saxon usage, and it is 'pet-e-rŏl' and not 'benzin' that makes the wheels go round.

Next in line for 'pet-e-rŏl' was an Afghan lorry, one of a noble race whose brightly painted bodywork and towering superstructures added fantasy to the humdrum highways ahead of us. On a standard chassis, probably imported from America via Karachi, the Afghan constructs (or rather has constructed for him by the Pakistani craftsmen in Peshawar), a slatted wooden body of

totally disproportionate height designed to contain the maximum
of goods or people. It is traditional for these lorries to be brightly
decorated (also undertaken in Peshawar), in the gaudy colours of
popular art—reds, greens, yellows and blues. This lorry was a particularly fine example of its breed. The driver's cabin was lined
with cut glass mirrors and hung with bright bobbles of silk.
Pictures were painted over every inch of surface, inside and out,
representing such innocent subjects as an Arcadian landscape with
a stream and poplars (a favourite subject in the folk art of thirsty
countries), a Joey-like parrot, a tiger and, as symbols of modernity
a telephone and a biplane. These devices seemed to recur on other
lorries and I imagine they could be ordered from a book of
patterns. We were to get to know them well and often recognized
old friends at various stages round the country by their markings.

We had lunch with Max and Mohamet Ali in a little restaurant
in the town. It was open on to the street and we soon became
objects of interest to the passers-by. There were carpets hanging
on the walls and wooden benches and tables crowded with
turbaned Afghans. This was my first introduction to their custom
of eating without utensils, an art I never really mastered despite
many attempts. It does not matter if you spill food on the table,
but I was anxious to avoid pouring it all over my lap. And if you
are inexpert this is by no means easy to avoid. The basic method
is to make a mixture of rice and meat or whatever you happen to
be eating in the palm of your hand and then, inclining the first
three fingers towards the mouth, to use the thumb to push it in.
It is a social solecism to use the left hand which is, in theory,
reserved for purposes connected with personal hygiene. The
problem of eating soup without a spoon is overcome by filling
the bowl with broken bread and scooping out the resultant soggy
mess. I asked Mohamet Ali why it was that the Afghans did not
use spoons, pointing out that it could hardly be because they
were so backward, since a spoon was among the more primitive
instruments known to man. He thought that religion had something to do with it, based on the supposition that food was the
gift of God, and that by interposing a man-made article between
it and your lips you were somehow detracting from the essential
virtue of the food. He was also of the opinion that it tasted better
that way.

After our quite unspiritual dish of mutton and rice we were

served a watery ice-cream with the rather sickly flavour of roses. Max said that Afghan ice-cream was invariably flavoured with roses and that he preferred the everlasting taste of roses to the wider range of flavours available in other countries. This remark was by way of being mildly controversial and was a specimen of Max's often-expressed rejection of certain aspects of Western civilization, which he delighted to compare unfavourably to Afghanistan. For example, when Diana said how much she had liked Salzburg, he came out with disparaging references to 'all that terrible tinkly music', yet he was consistently enthusiastic about Afghan music and we were made to listen to indifferent tape recordings he had made on his trips round the country. Max had lately been to Tashkent, Soviet Russia's showpiece in the south, and he observed how happy all the Russian peasants appeared to be compared with France and Spain. But I do not think Max was 'political'; he was not especially trying to subvert Mohamet Ali; his attitude seemed more that of an idealistically-inclined undergraduate. Max was a sensitive, intelligent person and we liked him very much.[1]

After lunch Mohamet Ali took us round the bazaar (a composite word for the many streets lined with open-fronted shops, simple, one-roomed constructions, propped up by wooden posts, in which there was barely space for the merchant to squat among his wares.) The intriguing peepshows, with their multiplicity of unfamiliar goods, were a joy and a delight to our inexperienced eyes and we were sorry to hear that all over Afghanistan the old bazaars were being pulled down in the name of hygiene and progress. Already in Herat piles of rubble marked the destruction of several acres prior to rebuilding on a more practical, if less picturesque, pattern.

I bought Diana a square of Indian silk to cover her shoulders, which seemed to be attracting a great deal of attention. A large crowd had surrounded us and bird-bright eyes were watching her every move. It was not every day they saw a lady without a veil, with bare legs and shoulders and a wisp of pale blue sack dress. Fierce-looking policemen lay into the goggling onlookers with curses, whacking indiscriminately and ferociously with wide

[1] Max took the opportunity of taking photographs during his scythe-selling trips, and his superb results have been recently published: *Afghanistan* by Flinker, Kessel & Klimburg. Thames & Hudson, 1959.

leather belts. This dispersal of crowds is probably done with the best intentions on the instructions of some ministry in Kabul, but I should say they were best left alone: if the Western visitor can afford such simple pleasure in uneventful lives he should feel gratified.

While Mohamet Ali bargained for blankets on our behalf I got into conversation with one of the crowd, an intelligent young man who said in English: 'I am a Jew.' He told me that there were several hundred Jews in Herat, but there would not be much longer for at last they were off to Israel. He was going in a week's time and would be glad to see the last of Herat. Herat was a 'dirty place! Life would be different in Haifa'. There seemed to be a certain anti-Jewish prejudice in Afghanistan, for Diana told me that Mohamet Ali had said to her: 'Doesn't he realize that is a Jew he is talking to?'

14

THE SOUTHERN ROUTE

'TRAVELLING is better when it takes place at night.' Amanullah, the hotel secretary, had insisted. 'In the daytime it is more sensible to remain in the shade. (Amanullah had a pedantic style of English acquired from phrasebooks and *Readers' Digests*. A few lessons from a cockney traveller had played havoc with his pronunciation. 'Mister Alexander,' he said gravely, 'Oy think that to improve moy English it will be necessary to speak as much as possible with English people.')

Just before our morning departure for Kabul I was tapping out on the hotel piano Noël Coward's song about Mad Dogs and Englishmen going out in the midday sun, when Amanullah came up and asked me to repeat the words. It was then that he came out with his advice. We saw what he meant after the shady avenue of pines that led for a surprisingly long way out of the town gave us up to the full glare of the sun. It was hotter than we had yet experienced and the fumes of the Russian petrol induced a nausea that was made critical by the merciless surface of the road. There was nothing to be seen except sand and stones. We suffered this for about eight hours until we sighted the green oasis of Farah, where the road turned round towards the east.

The wide blue river was spanned by a splendid bridge carried on iron girders. But a barrier lay across our path and I saw that construction was barely completed and that the concrete on the road had not yet set. There must have been a ford before this bridge was built, so I drove down to the stony river bank to find a crossing-place. A hundred yards away I saw what looked like a meeting place of tracks entering the broad waters, but we never reached it for the car got stuck in a tributary. Though narrow, it was fast flowing and filled with boulders; the more I tried to get out the deeper the wheels dug in. Two flat tyres were now added to our miseries.

There was not even the most vicarious pleasure to be found in our predicament. Dripping with sweat we heaved and excavated and revved, only to sink further into the shallows. The sun was like a scourge and we had run out of drinking water. I scooped up a handful from the stream, not caring that it had recently run through the town. At once my mouth began to shrivel up, fur sprouted on my lips and teeth and my tongue began to fizz and foam. I could not think what had happened until I realized that the water was full of alkali. Desperately spitting fire I staggered off to look for help.

A long line of Afghans were resting in the shade under the bridge. They must have seen that we were stuck, but nobody had answered my shouts. As I walked down the line of shirkers each one, as I came to him, got up on to his knees and ostentatiously began bowing and scraping in the direction of Mecca, thereby absolving himself from any obligation to help a distressed traveller. I cannot in the least blame them for not stirring on that baking afternoon, and at least they did not take offence, and even looked amused, when I made faces at them and said, 'Allah! Allah!' with as much contempt as I could muster.

At the very end of the line I came upon a young Afghan who was not praying, but was actually working. This industrious apprentice was hammering out a large tank; when I came to him he looked up sympathetically; then he got to his feet and had me follow him saying 'Jeep! Jeep!'

We forded the river and climbed up the opposite bank to arrive among a corral of bulldozers and other mechanical equipment that had been used in the construction of the bridge. I followed my guide into a hut marked KEEP OUT and there inside was a man wearing a sort of stetson hat, an open-necked shirt, and neatly-cut riding breeches. He had a small moustache and looked like a film actor of the vintage of Douglas Fairbanks Senior.

'I know. Don't tell me!' he said. 'Stuck in the river!'

His name was Joe Martell and he was the boss of the construction company which had built the bridge. We were standing in the tool-room and the walls were covered with pigeon-holed spares. 'We have to keep an eye on this stuff,' Joe said, 'there are a lot of very quick fingers in these parts.' He had a trace of French accent, and was in fact of French extraction though he had been born in California.

He sent a rescue party over in his smart new jeep to fetch Diana and to deal with the tyres. The hauling out could come later . . . meanwhile we must be feeling in need of a drink 'over at the camp'.

The camp was a collection of large trailers. Following Joe into the largest we were struck by a blast of refrigerated air. Each trailer had individual air conditioning from a plant that effectively cooled the air by circulating it over water sunk in a hole in the ground. We were in the Mess trailer, which was equipped with a shiny white cooking range and a large Frigidaire. We sat down at the table and Joe said the words I had been waiting for: 'What are you going to drink?' Before I could reply I was indiscriminately sampling king-sized cans of pineapple juice, tomato juice, milk, vegetable soup, beer, all ice-cold from the Frigidaire. I drank and drank and drank.

When Diana and I were satiated Joe said, 'What about a swim?' and in company with a German doctor and the Afghan chief engineer we went down to the river again. Joe was in great form and we amused ourselves by turning into rafts and floating down-stream on the current. Diana, looking very brown in her white bathing dress, drew even the formerly unco-operative Afghans from out of their shelter under the bridge.

Joe asked us to stay the night, and we were glad to accept his invitation. In company with his four colleagues, one of whom was a Filipino, we dined on soup, fish, fried steak and chocolate cake. 'We do ourselves as best we can,' said Joe, 'or else this sort of job would get you down. Poor Sam, over there, he's feeling a bit got down.' 'Poor Sam' was a morose American who had hardly opened his mouth throughout the meal. He was hard to please. He was shortly transferring to a job on one of the dams in the Elburz. When I suggested that he would have a fine time in Teheran he replied gloomily that the only point in doing the sort of job he was doing was the money you got and the fact that you were compelled to save it. In Teheran he might be tempted to spend it.

Tomorrow was a three-day holiday, the Moslem equivalent of Christmas, and Afghans from the camp were always turning up at the door of the trailer to ask for an extra day so that they could visit their families in some remote part of the country. Joe and the German doctor were planning to set off for a few days' 'leave' in Herat. We did not take very kindly to this German, who was arrogant and argumentative and very offhand with the Afghans.

'We Germans are the only people liked in this country,' he said.
'They despise the Americans and detest the British!' This remark,
made in the middle of dinner, passed without challenge, though
I was strongly tempted to say that if all the Germans in Afghanistan were like him they would soon find themselves at the bottom
of the popularity poll. I contented myself with saying that I had
heard they still had pictures of Hitler hanging up in the tea houses.

In our sleeping quarters—an air-conditioned trailer complete
with bunks and a shower—there were indications that a previous
occupant had been displaced. *True Detective* lay on my bedside
table; in the bathroom was a fine collection of aids to civilized
living in outlandish places which I chronicle, not to give these
products a free plug, but because I was fascinated by their names:
*Colgate Instant Barber Shave (aerosol lather). Beau Kreml Hair Tonic.
Scotch Heather 'Seaforth' After-Shave Lotion. Wildroot Cream Oil Hair
Tonic. Veto Spray Deodorant. Mennen After-Shave Talc Lotion for
Men. Prell Radiant Shampoo. Mennen Quicksana (for fungus infection
of the foot). Zest Deodorant Beauty Bar. Stim-U-Dents ('finish what the
toothbrush leaves undone')* . . . Perhaps they were Sam's, and our
occupation of his quarters had contributed to his tantrums.

Next morning, after spraying myself with 'Veto' and finishing
what my toothbrush had left undone, we joined Joe and the
German doctor for a dawn breakfast of ham and eggs. Then they
set off in the direction of Herat and we continued on the long
trail to Kabul.

It was another desperately hot day, and we drove through the
same shimmering cardboard hills. An old man with a long white
beard was hobbling along the stony verge. He waved his stick
tremulously, inviting us to stop and give him a lift. But he
looked too old to sit on the bonnet seat and Diana said that if
he was to come inside there was so much baggage that he would
have to sit on her lap which, understandably, was more than she
could face at that moment. So I drove on without stopping,
though suddenly filled with guilt and misgiving. As we passed
him, the old man lifted his hand and made some sinister cabalistic
sign, spat, and shrieked a quavering Islamic oath. I said to Diana:
'We ought to have given that old man a lift. Now he has put a
curse on us and you will see that we have bad luck of some sort.'
I was not really surprised when about three miles further on a

hateful slewing of the wheel indicated that we had a puncture. The curse was working quickly but with any luck it was only a small curse: it was no great effort to change the wheel and we could have the tyre fixed at Dilaram, which should not be more than a few miles ahead.

I was about to put on the spare wheel when I realized that it too was flat, though it had just been repaired by Joe's men at Farah. I was now faced with the prospect of mending a puncture myself, a task I found almost impossible because I could never manage to force the tyre from the rim, let alone get it back on again. On the previous occasion I had attempted the operation I had struggled for three hours before rescue arrived in the form of an Iranian lorry driver.

After a truly agonizing struggle I managed to get the tyre off. Then came the business of mending the puncture. I propose to treat this puncture question at some length once and for all: they had become something of an obsession by that time and by the end of the journey Diana estimated that we had had fifty-seven, though in fifty-five cases I was fortunate to find somebody to mend them. On getting a flat tyre somewhere in the middle of nowhere it became a desperate gamble to find help before the spare went, too. Usually we managed to reach a tea house or village, or perhaps a passing lorry driver would offer his services. The lorry drivers in Afghanistan and Persia showed extraordinary kindness on all occasions, stopping voluntarily if they saw we were in trouble and sometimes spending long hours getting us going again. They were knights of the road indeed, and we tried to make up for it by giving people lifts whenever possible. But this time I knew there would be no lorry driver: on this road they had the good sense to travel by night.

The only puncture outfits obtainable east of Istanbul are of a type unfamiliar to English drivers. They are imported from America and the most popular make in Afghanistan have a picture of a camel on the box, a close relation to the one on the cigarette packet. In the box are about a dozen tiny tin trays, each containing a wad of impregnated cardboard or *papiermâché*. The rubber patch is attached to the underside of the tin tray. An additional piece of equipment is necessary for the repair operation —a small vice. The method is to fit the bottom of the tin tray over the puncture, apply the vice over the whole, and tighten as hard as you can. Then comes the exciting part, which Diana usually insisted on doing. Light the impregnated pad and with luck it will start to smoke and hiss and smell like a firework. Blow on it and a red hot line fizzles across, providing heat to vulcanize the rubber. After a wait of a minute or two (it is tempting to act prematurely) unscrew the vice and delicately remove the tin tray. A beautiful new-born blue patch should now be revealed in position.

On this occasion, when I had done all the dirty work, Diana stood by with a match. She struck it with a flourish and applied it to the pad. It failed to ignite. This was because she had not followed the little trick of the professionals, who make a small nick in the pad where the match is to be applied. It happened to be the last match.

As usual, whenever anything went wrong, I began to swear at Diana: 'It's all your fault. We could easily have given that old man a lift and then this would never have happened. There's plenty of room in front!' Diana said nothing, knowing too well what heat and bumpy roads could do to my temper. But the poor girl could do no right. 'For goodness' sake say something! Don't just sit there and look hurt!' I raved, and felt the old man's poison go coursing through my veins.

The curse was almost expended. Walking to the top of the rise I saw the two buildings that were Dilaram no more than half a mile ahead. Leaving the car where it stood I began trundling a wheel up the road.

Almost dropping with heat and exhaustion I staggered to the door of a square building where a group of Afghans were squatting in the shade. *Hypocrite lecteur*, I ask you to believe that sitting in front was that horrible bearded old man we had passed at least six miles back on the road. You may say that bearded old Afghans all look alike, but I am certain it was he, for he shook his head knowingly up and down in a 'what did you expect' sort of way, and made no effort to help the others who immediately began to repair the wheel. How did he get there? No other vehicle had passed that way and he could hardly have taken a short cut as the road was absolutely straight.

Throughout Afghanistan, government rest houses are sited at strategic intervals. They are cheap and clean with carpeted floors and iron beds and usually a tank of water with a can. Dilaram

consisted of two buildings, one containing a battery-run trans-
mitting set, which no doubt reported our arrival and departure,
and the other the guest-rooms. Deciding that Amanullah's advice
about daytime travel should be respected, we took a room,
ordered a continual supply of tea, and flopped down on the beds.

The busy bearer of tea was a courteous 'gentleman's gentleman'
type. (Tea in Afghanistan is served in pretty little round china
teapots with cups to match, more gracious than in Turkey where
it comes in large glasses and more generous than Persia where it
comes in small glasses. Marks revealed that the main source of
supply was Japan and Russia.) From his hollow cheeks, yellow
skin and beaded brow, I guessed he was in the grip of fever.
Indeed, before we left he told us he was suffering from malaria
and asked if we could give him some medicine. We had a good
supply of Paludrin pills and he gratefully accepted a handful. It
was difficult to make him understand how many he had to take
and how often.

After a protracted siesta and a swim in the river behind the
hill, we prepared to set off again. The sun was now sinking and
the worst of the day was over.

It was dark when we came to Gerischt on the Helmand River. I
planned to stay there for the night, and early the following morning to look over the Ghaznavid ruins. I also wanted to see something of the 'Helmand Valley Project'. This grandiose scheme,
inaugurated with American aid, was an attempt to repeat the
success of the Tennessee Valley development project and turn a
vast area of desert in south-west Afghanistan into a fertile Eden.
Unfortunately their visionary plans had overlooked the fact that
the earth of the region was salty and intractable: despite the
irrigation it was refusing to yield a crop. And now, according to
the story I had heard at Joe Martel's camp, it had just been found
that the concrete-lined canal bringing the river through the
turbines had sprung so many leaks that there was not sufficient
weight of water to drive the wheels.

It was the Moslem equivalent of Christmas night and the little
town was filled with festive crowds. We stopped at a *chai-khana*
to listen to a group of musicians playing outside. Their performance was infinitely more exciting than anything I had heard on
Max's tape recorder and I wished he had been there to listen.

The main work was scored for two voices, baritone and counter-tenor, the high part being sung by a boy whose voice was not a treble so much as an uncanny liquid falsetto. The deeper voice would sing one verse and the youth would reply with the next, with occasional passages of close harmony that resembled Monte-verdi. The accompaniment came from the usual Afghan trio—finger drum, stringed instrument and pipe.

I asked a character standing on the edge of the crowd if he could tell me the way to the hotel, or rest house. He greeted my question with enormous enthusiasm and jumped on to the car crying 'Otel Amrica! Otel Amrica!' and pointing ahead into the darkness. I took this to mean that there was an American hotel (a junior Hilton?) just down the road. Six hours and a hundred and fifty miles later we arrived at Kandahar with our guide still insisting that it lay immediately ahead.

There *was* a hotel and it was called the Hotel de Kandahar, but it was full up and we had to sleep on mattresses on the floor in the large lounge. Our optimistic guide from Gerischt, who gave his name as Raouf, had attached himself firmly to us; he had organized us into the hotel and now expressed himself anxious to attend to our needs wherever we intended to go—Kabul, Inglestan, Amrica, anywhere! He insisted on sleeping on the balcony beside the car and I resolved at least to retain him for the journey round the north, where an attendant tyre-changer might well come in useful. Next morning I put him to work running errands in the town. It is true that he tried to cheat me of one hundred afghanis on the morning's trading—when challenged he produced the odd excuse that he had given the money to a friend to look after and would immediately go and get it—but he made up for this by cleaning out the car without being asked. To tell the truth I felt proud of having a retainer of my own!

Kandahar was the second town of Afghanistan and the hotel was the centre of its social web. In the morning we met two Scandinavian diplomats who had driven up from Karachi to escape the heat (as the temperature in Kandahar was over 110 degrees I dread to think what it must have been like in Karachi). We also met the young Afghan manager of the airport and several trainee pilots of the recently created *Air Ariana*, Afghanistan's own airline, formed under the auspices of Pan-American. These young men, looking fit and handsome in their blue overalls with

an orange ARYANA across their backs, had recently passed their
B licence and were shortly off to the States for further training.
It was hoped that Kandahar would become the most important
communications centre in air traffic between Asia and Europe.

Before lunch I left Diana in charge of a charming young
Afghan called Abdul Aziz and went off to pay a call on the headquarters of Morison Knudsen, the great firm of American engineers who were the power behind most of the construction work in
progress in Afghanistan. MK, as they were known, had been
responsible for the Helmand River project and it was to find out
more about this apparent débâcle, with a view to writing an
article for the British Press, that I had decided to visit them,
despite their reputation for not welcoming casual visitors with
entirely open arms.

The MK headquarters was in a vast enclosure, like a state
within a state, on the edge of the town. It was surrounded by a
high wire fence and floodlights were placed at intervals round the
perimeter. Passing the guard at the gate I found myself in an
enormous car park of miscellaneous vehicles ranging from Cater-
pillar tractors to the latest Chrysler. Escorted by an old Afghan
in a topee I went to look for the Public Relations Officer, the
most likely person to handle difficult inquiries such as mine.
Within the compound were numbers of little houses each with
its own lawn, and garden growing such homely vegetables as
lettuce, sweet corn and cabbages. People were sitting in deck
chairs on their porches and I shyly tried several recumbent figures
without being able to find the right person.

In the centre of the compound was a swimming pool from
whence tantalizing girlish shouts such as 'leave off pulling my
pants, willya!' beckoned irresistibly and I rather awkwardly
approached the group of men, women and children disporting
there. I talked to a gentle grizzled man, who showed no evidence
of the inhospitality I had been led to expect and suggested I
come in for a dip, taking me back to his little house and fitting
me up with a costume.

It was a happy gathering and I felt sorry for Diana left behind
in the stuffy hotel. A pretty Japanese (?) lady asked me to stay
for lunch and after a game of water polo with the young, I went
back to her house for a delicious meal of tuna fish prepared with
a salad from her garden. Her American husband, one of MK's

specialists in road construction, donned a blue kimono and sat at ground level in the approved Oriental fashion. When I said that what I had heard about MK's lack of hospitality did not seem true my host replied that any such suggestion was due to the fact that the management found it difficult to justify 'entertainment of sundry travellers' on the balance sheet, which was paid by the Afghan government. My friends thought it regrettable that company policy was not more liberal in this respect bearing in mind the small number of people likely to be involved. 'Public relations' would surely have made an appropriate entry on the accounts, and entertainment of travellers was a tradition that Afghans understood.

This ambivalence with the Afghan government was further brought out when, after lunch, I met the PRO. When I asked him about the Helmand River project he said that he was unable to make statements on company matters unless he first cleared it with Afghan representatives in the organization. He added that if I cared to talk to them—and he did not think they would be around until after the holiday—he would arrange a meeting. It hardly seemed worth while waiting several days on the offchance of getting interesting information out of reluctant Afghans, so I said I would call in again next time I passed that way. The unofficial impression I obtained elsewhere from MK men was that responsibility lay with the Afghan government experts who were apt to be over-confident in their own engineering abilities.

We left Kandahar as soon as the sun began to go down, with Raouf outriding on the bonnet. I went on driving until midnight when I stopped and went to sleep over the wheel. Diana made herself more or less comfortable on the petrol cans in the back and, girding his dirty robes around him like a chrysalis, Raouf curled up in the road. Before the sun rose again we drove on, stiff and cold and very unsettled inside.

The next stepping-stone on the road to Kabul is Ghazni, former capital of a great empire, and in its day (twelfth and thirteenth centuries) a rival to the glories of Baghdad. The glory had certainly departed but there were notable ruins at Ghazni and to pay them our respects we turned off the main road and headed for the citadel above the town. From that eminence I hoped to see exactly where the ruins were located.

We crossed a fine old bridge, thronged with people, for this was still a time of holiday. The dried-up river bed was a scene of gaiety and animation: a children's fair was in progress with simple swings and merry-go-rounds upon which enchanting children dressed in their colourful best were furiously whirling. I was taking a photograph of a little boy wearing the traditional red velvet waistcoat stitched with gold, who bore a young hawk on his wrist, when the inevitable chocolate-uniformed police arrived and began to lay about them with their belts. At the same time they asked for our papers and tried to make me hand over the camera. I made signs that I only wanted to photograph the children and thanks to Raouf's intervention I was allowed to continue.

Continuing across the bridge we climbed a steep hill and passed a barracks outside which some ancient field guns were ornamentally arrayed, still pointing in the direction from which the British Army approached in the First Afghan War on their way from Quetta to Kabul. We stopped in a small square with a fine view over the lower town and the surrounding countryside. From the citadel above came the sound of martial music: the local regiment was apparently giving a concert to the citizens. I was looking for the ruins through my field-glasses when some soldiers came running up and began shouting in a typically Teuton way (the Afghan Army was once trained by the Germans and still wears the *stahlhelm* and jackboot). They wanted us to come with them down the hill and when I refused they returned with an officer, who went through the familiar routine of checking papers. Then two more officers arrived and we were ordered to drive to the barracks below.

At the barracks Raouf, despite my protests, was hustled away between two soldiers with fixed bayonets and we waited anxiously in the courtyard while various people came up and examined our passports.

At last we were taken into the barracks; into a small room with six rugged officers sitting round a table. It was the Turkish affair all over again.

This time questions were put through a young civilian who had been called in for the occasion. What were we doing up there? Looking for the ruins . . . Why was I photographing the bridge; did I not know it was forbidden to take photographs?

I was not photographing the bridge, I was photographing the children under the bridge and the police had permitted it . . . Had we not seen the notice NO ENTRY by the barracks? Yes, I had seen the notice, but it clearly referred to the barracks itself and not to the road going past it. (They were forced to agree this was so) . . . Who was the man we were travelling with? I told them how we had met Raouf in Gerischt.

Then came a complication. 'That is not the story the man has told us,' they said. 'He says his name is Ghavour. I am afraid you will not be able to take him with you any further. He has no identity card and will be returned to Kandahar under arrest.' I insisted that Raouf, Ghavour, Gunga Din, or whatever his name was must come with me. He was my servant and my responsibility; on no account would I abandon him. It was then quietly pointed out to me that it was against the law to be without an identity card in Afghanistan. 'Ghavour' had committed a crime, and if he could not produce his card soon he would be liable to punishment. If he could produce his card, which he said he had left at home, then all would be well. If not . . .

In the opinion of the Afghan officers he was trying to shirk his military service. 'He is not a man!' they cried disdainfully. Then Raouf (or Ghavour) was brought in. He regarded me shamefacedly and seemed resigned to his fate. I gave him a few afghanis and wished him luck. I think he was a rogue, and it is likely we should have had trouble with him had he accompanied us further.

A report had to be made to Kabul. I was made to sign the statement they had laboriously taken down. They wanted to leave out the bit about the sign NO ENTRY referring only to the barracks' gate, since it took away any real grounds for our arrest. But though willing to help I explained that I did not want to have a bad mark against my name so soon and prejudice my chances of travelling in the north. The officers were anxious to make amends for our long detention: a meal of *pilau*, and what they described as an Afghan speciality, but was in fact no more than slimy semolina, was set before us. Then we asked if we could see the ruins, and the interpreter, who turned out to be an employee in the Ministry of Agriculture, offered to show us round.

After we had looked at the ornate Ghaznavite towers— Mahmud's Towers of Victory—each with a corrugated iron hat to keep the weather out, our charming young guide, who had taken a fancy to Diana and asked if he could call her 'sister', invited her to call on his fifteen-year-old fiancée, who lived nearby. He intended to have no more than one wife, he was anxious to explain: it was only uneducated Afghans who had more. I had to wait outside while they went into the little house where she lived. Diana reported she was quite pretty and wore a shapeless cotton dress. Her name, Spozhmai, meant 'Moon', and she was pleased to learn that 'Diana' also had lunar associations.

15

KABUL

THE LAST ninety odd miles to Kabul, even without shock absorbers, could be enjoyed for an increasing beauty in the surrounding country. Deep, clear streams now watered a landscape squared with young rice and corn of burnished gold; pale green poplars in long vertical glades grew so close together that not even the slimmest deer could run through them. As the sun went down the previously *papiermâché* hills seemed to lose their volume and become paper thin, stepping back like a drawing lesson in shaded, receding planes, as sharply etched as silhouettes. Then Kabul came into sight ringed with purple mountains and the last rays of the sun splintered over it with the bravura of a Bach toccata. If my prose also has taken on a purple tinge, I feel the scene demands it.

A straight tarred road took us into an urban world of concrete, cars, buses and a skyline scarred with telephone wires. 'OTEL? OTEL?' we shouted at all the passers-by, and though we tried every combination of inflexions we were answered by blank uncomprehending stares. Whether they were genuinely uncomprehending or simply registering disapproval of our unceremonious manner of address, was never established. We were wandering round the darkening streets in a daze when a Rover saloon drew up alongside and the traditional, 'Can I be of any help?' came from within. 'We are looking for a hotel!' we cried, and the voice replied, 'You'd better come along with me first.' A few minutes later we were following a short, sandy man to a large white villa, through the door and into a spacious hall with a dartboard on the far wall. 'Ethel!' shouted our guide and a kind-looking lady greeted us in a motherly way and insisted we stay for supper. Our host was Mr Lord, and he ran a school of sanitation under the auspices of the World Health Organization. 'The Afghans have a lot to learn,' he said, when I brought to his notice the only lavatory we had so far met, the defective 'Little Niagara' in Herat. Mrs Lord produced a delicious supper of bacon, eggs, sausages and her special cake. She said she would 'love a nice salad' but the local lettuces were 'full of worm's eggs and however much you washed them you couldn't get rid of them'. So she made lettuce soup instead.

The Lords were discouraging about our proposed journey to the north. 'They're all barbarians up there,' said Mrs Lord and brought up the old case of Winant and the Swedish girl. 'Mark my words, lust was at the bottom of that!' added Mr Lord.

After showing us his fine collection of Afghan carpets Mr Lord guided us in his Rover to the Hotel Kabul. It stood next to a fine lit-up showroom filled with the electrical products of the German firm of Siemens. 'They put in all the lighting in Kabul,' said Mr Lord, rather resentful that it had not been a British firm, 'so it's little wonder they have a monopoly of the fittings.'

We booked into the fusty, fussy hotel with the depressing feeling that though we seemed to have been on the road for years we had achieved no more than half our journey.

Our tour of inspection of the town the next morning started badly. The slit-eyed driver of the *gaudi*[1] prodded his highly-decorated horse just as Diana had her foot on the step and caused her to fall flat on her face in the street. For the rest it was an uncomfortable trip even on the good Russian-built tarred roads and we had to sit on a very hard and narrow seat with our backs to the horse in continual danger of bouncing off.

The social life of the town seemed to be centred on, or rather in, the rapidly drying-up river that ran through the middle: it was lido, lavatory and laundry—women washed, boys bathed, animals drank and performed their natural functions in its festering shallows. Behind was the bazaar, hiding as if ashamed behind the more pretentious buildings that lined the three main streets, but that day, being *Jummah*, it was shut. Government offices, embassies and the private houses of the rich spread out in the eastern suburbs. Occasional 'follies' built by King Amanullah, Afghanistan's unsuccessful Atatürk, diverted the eye. Amanullah had a craze for architecture and borrowed freely from all sources. Perhaps his most extraordinary effort was an octagonal building by the river, with no apparent function, which is said to be based on a building in Bayswater; it was known locally as Little London.

[1] A smart little pony-trap made in Peshawar. Along with Russian buses labelled CITY BUS they form the public transport of Kabul.

Another remarkable object was the Maiwand war memorial, a bright blue rocket-like obelisk constructed in smart World Fair style. This monument, at the intersection of busy streets, commemorated the defeat of the British General Burrows in 1881. It was to relieve his army that General Roberts executed his famous march from Kabul to Kandahar (384 miles) in twenty-three days. A second monument, a tall column flanked by field guns, stood at the end of a wide ceremonial avenue called Istiqlal Wat and commemorated Afghan Independence as established by the Treaty of Rawalpindi in 1919. ('Of course you will be attending the Independence Day celebrations on August the first,' Amanullah had said in Herat. 'Independence from what?' I asked innocently. 'From you Breetish!' Amanullah had replied gleefully.)

After an hour of such haphazard impressions the *gaudi* dropped us back at the hotel for lunch. In the dining-room we sat down next to sixteen Soviet citizens whose sixteen panama hats hung from a hatstand like rare fruits on a tree. They did not have much to say to each other, but they looked sincere and serious. Later, having my papers stamped at the police station, I counted sixteen green passports with CCPR engraved on the front.

In the afternoon I paid a call on the British Embassy. There were several reasons for my visit: to take a look, to get a new passport (owing to the amount of writing officials indulge in east of Istanbul my old one was full), to notify the Consul that I was heading north and to be ready to bail me out if I got into any trouble, to have the car repaired in the Embassy garage, and to collect mail.

The Embassy lies conveniently out of riot-range, about three miles outside the town. A sweeping drive curves up to a pillared residence built in the best Curzonian tradition. According to the custom of polite travellers I presented myself at its portals to write my name in 'the book', in the hope of getting at least an invitation to tea. The door was opened by a Pakistani butler, impeccably dressed *à l'anglaise*, who bowed with dignity and regretted that 'the book' was at that moment undergoing inspection at the Chancellery, and could I come back tomorrow. As I turned sadly away I caught a tantalizing glimpse of a polished hall, a black spaniel, a Constance Spry arrangement of flowers; as I drove off a thick-legged girl (Miss Hunter Dunn?) in white shorts crossed the beautiful lawn with a tennis racquet under her arm and a string bag of balls dangling at her side.

The Chancellery and Consulate were set to one side in a long low building. The Embassy staff lived in surrounding villas built in the uncompromisingly suburban style of East Sheen. The First Secretary rather proudly told me that an article in the *Scotsman* had described the Embassy as 'brooding intellectually'. I must confess that I had the impression, after one or two visits, that 'squatting smugly' would have been a more appropriate metaphor.

There are no proper garages in Kabul, so visiting GB motorists are forced to beg help from the Embassy garage, who, if not too busy, do their best to help at a reasonable price. I had bought my car, a 1951 Land Rover, in the upper reaches of the King's Road for £265. 'Are you certain it is reliable? I have to take it on a long trip,' I had said to the odiously confidential salesman. 'I'd personally guarantee this car any day,' he had replied enthusiastically. 'I'd drive it up to Scotland and back tomorrow!' Except for minor matters it had served us well, but this seemed the moment for those minor matters to be dealt with. While it was being attended to under the shade of a giant mulberry ('them things are breakfast, dinner and tea to the people in this country,' said the head mechanic) a tall ginger-moustached figure in check coat, cavalry twill trousers and ginger suede shoes came over and inspected the proceedings. He introduced himself as the Military Attaché, a fact that I had already surmised. When I told him I was writing a book and asked if he could give me any information about conditions in the north he retired behind a defensive position. 'Oh no. You're not going to get anything out of me! Once bitten, twice shy! Some damned writer, he was an MP too, quoted me saying a lot of things I never said. If I was to meet the fellow at the door of my club, I'd kick him down the stairs!' 'May I quote you on *that*?' I said, mentally filing this rare remark. He then saw that he had over-committed his forces and that this could be another case where the pen was mightier than the protocol. 'Come round to my office, sometime, and we'll have a talk,' he compromised. But when I poked my nose in the following day, he did not seem in a mood that encouraged conversation, which was a pity as I should have liked him to have continued his history lesson. His preamble was promising: 'These Afghans have got their history all wrong. Seem to think they

The Pool of the Five
Brothers, Bujnurd

Diana (in Turkoman
coat) and Boris in front
of his 1901 Russian
bathe

Mr Raj entertains at the former British Consulate, Meshed

A swimming party at the US Consulate, Meshed

won all the wars, and we started 'em. Can't make them see that wasn't the way it happened at all.'

I learnt from the American Consulate, who proved to be more helpful than the British in volunteering useful information, of the existence of the International Club, an institution that means much to a stranger in the city. It lies on the edge of the town beyond the Ladies' Work Association, which was the only establishment in Kabul besides Siemens with a window display, in this case some pretty needlework objects sewn by Afghan ladies. (I never got to see an Afghan lady in Kabul as they were always completely submerged, except for a long mesh window, in pleated tent-like veils of grey or blue or beige. I was told that if an Afghan lady appeared in the streets of Kabul without her veil, people would throw stones at her. But the moment the diplomats' wives get in the aeroplane for foreign parts their veils are off in a flash to reveal the latest elegant fashion.)

There was a swimming pool at the Club but our first visit coincided with the day it was being cleaned. Unlike the Hilton, it seemed to need it. There was an abominable detritus at the bottom compounded of innumerable dead flies, beetles and what Tony would have referred to as 'undesirable *algae*'. In addition there were several enormous toads, one of which a revolting little French boy was actually inflating with a straw.

People were drinking on the veranda. I approached an Anglo-Saxon type, who turned out to be a Swede, and asked how I could become an honorary member of the Club. I was passed on to an American, the honorary secretary, who passed me to the Afghan secretary. Having parted with my subscription I was issued with a book of tickets, which could be exchanged against drinks and food, and immediately disposed of forty-five afghanis' worth for a bottle of beer, imported from Germany, which was very refreshing despite the high price.

At lunch in the clubhouse we found ourselves sitting next to a disgruntled American from General Motors, newly arrived from the States, who had the task of collecting money owed to his company for trucks supplied over the past few years. Large numbers of these were apparently piling up at Karachi, where they would remain until somebody paid for them. The trouble was, he said, that the Afghan government, in a praiseworthy

5

attempt to stop profiteering, had set up a marketing agency working on a 15 per cent commission. As a result of this narrow margin
the distributors were broke and 'unable even to finance a cable
to New York'. 'If only the government wouldn't meddle in
business,' he complained, 'those trucks would be running on the
roads instead of sitting in those damn docks. People are crying
out for trucks in Afghanistan. It seems as how I shall have to be
out here at least six months clearing up the mess.'

The club notice board announced that there was to be a 'Gala
Tenth Anniversary' the following night—'Black Tie', 'Dancing',
'Barbecue'. In anticipation of imagined embassy receptions I had
packed a dinner jacket and Diana had a smart dress. This would
be an occasion for justifying their inclusion in our baggage.

We went with a sophisticated Swedish couple and a socially
insecure Indian in a high-collared black coat and white jodhpurs.
During the course of the evening I can remember meeting a gentleman on the Turkish Military Mission to the Afghan Army, a member of the 'Pakistan Archæological Mission', an Indian lady doctor
in a lilac sari, the Polish Ambassador, an Afghan prince, an
American professor of Pushtu at Kabul University, a Russian
ditto, and assorted Europeans of whom a large proportion were
Germans. 'There is more opportunity for young hard-working
Germans in this country than anywhere else,' said one, who
admitted that he found his opportunity illegally importing Mercedes cars and selling them on the Black Market.

There were coloured lights and dancing on the lawn, and a
sacrificial sheep on a burning pyre with pieces being hacked off
by sweating Afghan cooks. There was a Rock and Roll com-
petition, judged by the Polish Ambassador, which Diana was persuaded to enter by a tall, ill-co-ordinated German called Dietrich.
Though Diana is an expert, he was not, and as a team they were
hopelessly outclassed by a young American couple.

The American shop window in Kabul, the USIS or US Information Service, was dressed with photo-montages of the American
Way of Life: students on the campus, steelworkers in the steel
mill, senators in the Senate. Inside there were lecture rooms and
a library of books and magazines. The magazines were a disappointment: instead of the exciting glossies like *Vogue* and
Harpers', *Esquire* and others that give the stranger such a vivid

impression of a land of Milk and Honey, all I could find were inferior publications devoted to practical matters like wood-working, marine engineering and popular science.

The place was being made ready for a 'Civil Aviation Collo-quium', billed to take place that evening. A sourpuss woman organizer barked at an Afghan youth on his way to the library that 'this wasn't a public thoroughfare'. She said it in such an unpleasant way and the Afghan looked so surprised and hurt that I concluded she was more than undoing whatever goodwill might be engendered by the whole paraphernalia of the USIS. This lady was not in fact American but (I think) Swiss. She should in my opinion, be replaced, for it is charm rather than straight information that quiets the savage breast.

I sat in at the 'colloquium' which was well attended by the youth of Kabul, who seemed to listen with attentive interest to the speakers—Robert C. Green, Chief of the Civil Aviation Assistance Group; Colonel Mohammed Gul Bahar, Director-General of Afghan Civil Aviation; Ralph Mcguire, Civil Aviation Adviser, United States Operations Mission to Afghanistan, and Frank G. Swayze, Executive Vice-President, Aryana Air Lines.

Air Aryana, growing up under the auspices of Pan-American, seemed to be coming along nicely with the six aircraft (two DC4s and four DC3s) in their fleet; thanks to the pilgrim trade (2,400 *hajjis* went airborne to Jeddah), and the freighting of *caraculi* (new-born lamb) skins and sausage casings, they were actually running at a profit. There were great openings for the youth of Afghanistan, said Mr Robert C. Green, not only as pilots but on the many subsidiary jobs connected with getting an aeroplane into the air. In four to five years, Mr Frank G. Swayze estimated, Aryana Airlines would be run by the Afghans. 'We people are here just as long as it takes you people to get into the planes and into the pilots' seats. Then we go home . . .'

After such statements from the avuncular Americans on the stand, the youth of Afghanistan, as represented in that audience, looked appropriately starry-eyed.

Back at the hotel a man and a woman were talking in a con-spiratorial huddle at a table on the landing outside my bedroom. The woman had a note-book in her hand, and from her appear-ance—a combination of Eve Perrick and Iris Ashley—I guessed

'Fleet Street'. From her bazaar-made bag and cunning little Kabul shoes I guessed she must know her way around; and from her air of intense concentration and the determined play she made with her pencil, I guessed she must be on to a good story. I tried to listen through the door but could catch no more than a few personal pronouns on the wing; nor could Diana, whom I sent on several spying missions down the passage, contribute more than the fact that she thought that the man had an American accent.

I met the lady the following day at the office of Mr Tarzi, the charming Minister for Tourism. (I went to ask for permission to travel to the north, if possible as far as the Amu Darya, and to inquire about the exact locality of a recently discovered minaret near Herat which I had formed an ambition to visit.) 'I am afraid it is not possible at present to send you to Bamyan!' Mr Tarzi was saying to her plaintively. 'Perhaps when our organization is further advanced we will get one of those little buses to take people there on trips. We can run a tour to include our beautiful lakes of Band-i-Amir. The road is quite good. I was there recently. We have big plans for tourism in Afghanistan.'

Now I, too, wished to visit Bamyan, home of the two famous Giant Buddhas, on my way to the north. So I offered to take the lady with me if she could find her own way back. The Tourist Minister was greatly relieved by my offer as I think her persistence might have forced him to buy a little bus specially for her. In return he made no difficulties about providing me with a chit to the Ministry of the Interior in support of my application to travel the northern route. As regards the Amu-Darya—that was no concern of his, it was a military area. As regards the minaret he suggested I call on Mohamet Ali Kohzad, the president of the Historical Society of Afghanistan, who had an office down the passage.

The mystery lady now introduced herself as Stella Snead, and she was no reporter even if she 'did a bit of writing. None of it seems to get published, though'. The man she had been 'interviewing' in the passage was a recently arrived American, whom she had been trying to talk into accompanying her to Bamyan in his car. Stella had come out to Kabul by bus and lorry, and was now planning to go on to India. She was a charming lady and would make an agreeable companion among the Buddhas.

I found Mr Kohzad in his little office. All that I knew about my minaret, which had become for me a tangible objective in an excursion that seemed to lack a target, I had read in an article in the *Manchester Guardian* not long before my departure:

RELIC OF GLORY OF GHORI DYNASTY—MOSLEM MINARET IN REMOTE AFGHAN VALLEY

A member of the French Archæological Mission to Afghanistan, M. Maricq, has recently brought to light one of the noblest monuments of Moslem architecture, which seems to have attracted the attention of none but a few mountain shepherds for centuries past, though it is nearly 200 feet high —a minaret standing in a remote defile of the Hari Rud valley, just south of the Paropamisus mountains. The area is so little known that the river is marked only in dotted lines, having never been surveyed. The tower has lifted its slender length of amber-coloured masonry against a background of crag and snow-capped mountain since somewhere around AD 1170. The once-royal town in the neighbourhood, which M. Maricq had no time to visit, is apparently an uninhabited ruin.'

Though I was eager to see the 'slender length of amber-coloured masonry', I was even more interested in the 'once-royal town in the neighbourhood, which M. Maricq had no time to visit'. M. Maricq and all other members of the French Archæological Mission were away in France, but Mr Kohzad, though he had not been there, was able to tell me exactly where the minaret was located. He had in fact indicated its existence to M. Maricq, having heard reports of a tall tower beside the Hari Rud from travellers flying over it on the regular air service from Teheran to Kabul.

Mohamet Ali Kohzad talked enthusiastically about the ruined town that lay across the river. He strongly suspected that it might be the site of Firuzkoh, lost capital of the Ghori kings, whose empire had included Afghanistan and a great part of Persia and north-west India until it was overthrown by the Mongols under Ogotai, son of Genghiz Khan, sometime in the thirteenth century.

Having pointed out its position on the map, about 150 miles east of Herat, Mr Kohzad gave me a letter of introduction to the

Governor-General of the province. As I left his office he wryly showed me the gold-braided accoutrements of a Victorian Hussar officer, picked up on some battlefield of the Second Afghan War.

Except for getting permission to visit the Amu Darya, which a few test inquiries told me was likely to be a lengthy job, we were now ready to start for the north. As I paid our bill the manager asked what we thought of his hotel. I said I thought it was very nice. 'No, it is not nice at all,' he said sadly, 'but what can I do?' To Diana he whispered gallantly: 'You are the most beautiful girl who has ever been here. You are just my *teep*. If an Afghan woman is really beautiful she looks like you . . .'

Stella Snead turned up looking like Rose Macaulay in a nineteen-thirtyish skirt and stoically squashed into the desperately uncomfortable third seat. We drove out of town by a back way as I wanted to have a look at the enormous Russian-built silo said to be full of American grain, a nice example of Afghanistan's equal distribution of patronage between the rival powers. To regain the main road to the north it was necessary to cut across some difficult country. While we were negotiating an open ditch, a gentleman emerged from some poplar trees and wished us luck on our trip, pointing out that Bamyan lay in precisely the opposite direction to that in which we were heading. It was Mr Tarzi, the Tourist Minister.

16

BAMYAN

THE ROAD to the north begins its long climb to the top of the Hindu Kush even in the suburbs of Kabul. We drove out towards distant snow-peaks, through fertile valleys lined with poplars until the terrain became dramatically hacked with high-walled sun-excluding canyons. The road picked its way cautiously from one side of a rushing river to the other, seeking a foothold on the rocky edges of the ravine whenever the bottom proved too inhospitable. At 10,000 feet we reached the Shiba Pass. It was cold up there and our companion stream suddenly became deep and dark and sheered off through a grassy meadow to its glacial source.

Another river was born beyond the watershed to join the Amu Darya in the distant sands of Turkestan. We followed it for twenty miles and then it sent out a branch to the west. This was the Bamyan river and an arrowed sign at the road junction 'AFGHAN-TOURS—BAMYAN' bore useful witness to Mr Tarzi's activities.

It was dusk when we turned along the old Silk Road. The river, roaring along in its gorge to our left, shone with a strange luminosity. Grey forms and twisted phantoms seemed to people the rocks and ruined medieval keeps. Diana felt sure the valley was haunted, and local legend has it that this is so. But Stella was staunchly spirit-proof and kept us entertained with stories of her transcontinental travels as we bumped along the never-ending track. It was only twenty-five miles, but it seemed an age before we came upon long lines of tall poplars and followed one of these noble avenues to a white hotel upon a hill. Though they did not show themselves, we knew that somewhere nearby two giant Buddhas brooded in the dark.

We saw them the next morning from the windows of the hotel, sitting placidly in their niches in the wall of a great escarpment, their serene countenances smiling in the morning sun, one hundred and one hundred and thirty feet high respectively.

Along this valley the silk-laden caravans of China used to travel on their way to India. For eight centuries Bamyan sheltered communities of Buddhist monks; then Genghiz Khan came rampaging down from the north and destroyed the old city. But though the Buddhas have been hacked about they still stand comparatively intact.

After breakfast we went down to the little village that clustered round the foot of the escarpment and acquired a guide to show us round. He was a Hazara, slant-eyed descendant of the soldiers of Tamurlane. We followed panting up a steep slope and entered a door in the side of the rock; then came a climbing of innumerable crumbling stairs giving occasional glimpses through shafts in the sides of Buddha's mighty flanks. After passing through tunnelled passages and crossing rickety gangplanks we finally emerged on top of the Lord Buddha's very head, flat since it was scalped by infuriated Mongols revenging the murder of their prince some-where in the twelfth century.

The curving roof above was frescoed with happy scenes of birds and dancing ladies. We looked outwards over a wide valley backed by the snow-sprinkled mountains of the Hindu Kush. The sweet smell of the pea-fields wafted up to us and all manner of faraway sounds reached us through that still, clear air—the gentle purring of the rows of poplar, the chanting of children in the village school and the liquid flutings of a shepherd's pipe answered with a complementary refrain by a colleague in another field. The legendary Shangri-la might well have been sited in such a landscape as lay before us.

We climbed the second Buddha too, and visited a number of the little caves with which the cliff was honeycombed. They had once been occupied by the Buddhist priests and some were richly decorated with frescoes. But most were black with a thick bitu-minous substance that could be flaked off with the fingers, com-pounded of innumerable depositions of soot from the lamps and fires of former occupants.

Stella, indefatigable sightseer as she was, wanted to go on to the lakes of Band-i-Amir, sixty miles to the west, a group of deep mountain-ringed lakes of a deep blue colour and strongly recom-mended by Mr Tarzi. But every extra mile was a tax on thinning tyres and I was glad when a Turkish family, in an already over-laden car, bravely offered to take her with them.[1]

We abandoned Stella after lunch and returned down the track

[1] She subsequently wrote, in a letter postmarked PANCHATI, INDIA, 'I never got there! The station wagon of the Turkish people would not go up hills.'

Diana and the giant Budda, Bamyan

View from the Buddha's head, Bamyan : Hindoo Kush in background

we had taken the night before, getting two punctures in the process, but as usual finding help. It was dusk when we reached the main river again. In a gloomy ravine beside the rushing waters we were stopped by a phantom Afghan. He was carrying a sack of apricots and wanted a lift to his village. Before long he signalled us to stop, pointing urgently across the stream. I could just make out a haphazard collection of tents on a grassy ledge beside the water immediately backed by the mountain wall. Fires flickered in the half light. It was *kuchi*[1] encampment.

Our friend inclined his head sideways on his hands, pointing first at us and then towards the camp, as if to inquire whether we would care to spend the night there. We should have liked to very much, but I could see no possible means of crossing the river—a rapid yellow torrent over sixty yards wide, in which a ferryboat would have no chance of any movement other than downstream. I then thought we might have a demonstration in the use of inflated sheepskins such as I had read about in travel books. But it was simpler than that—removing his shirt to reveal a barrel-shaped body barely covered by a wisp of cotton, placing his clothes, his apricots and his shoes on the top of his head, our Afghan walked confidently into the waist-deep water without even testing it with his toe. He seemed to go at great speed, with a sort of gliding motion, running across and downstream at the same time, so that he reached the far side about thirty yards further down. It was an impressive performance, but strictly, we considered, for the experts.

He was now no more than a shadowy form in the gloom and we thought we had seen the last of him. But a minute or two later there was a sound of distant splashing and he came bounding back, this time with a bowl of yoghourt on his head, which he thrust into my hands and insisted that we eat. It was especially revolting, sour and crusted with dirt. But it was a kind thought and we made a great effort to get it down.

We now began to wonder where we were expected to stay the night. Our friend soon made it clear that he intended us to cross the stream to the encampment. Without further explanation he took Diana by the hand and led her into the water. She went over like a queen, without a moment's hesitation, dancing through the waves with one hand clinging to her guide. Though

[1] Nomads.

5*

soaked from top to toe she made the other side without a fall. Then the indefatigable Afghan returned for me. . . . It was a strange sensation, like running up a moving staircase going down, but not too difficult if you plunged forward fast enough; the moment you slowed down the current would begin to get a grip and threaten to throw you off balance.

A group of *kuchis* clustered round the landfall. Strong arms clutched, interested fingers plucked, starling voices discussed. More roots were thrown on to the fire and we went shivering towards it. They brought blankets and padded robes and urged me to sit near the fire. Diana, a mere woman, was quite ignored until I had been taken care of. Then a toothless beldame began to rub her down, and she too was given a blanket under which she took off all her clothes.

The men clustered round the fire; the women, mostly old hags or child brides of twelve or so, stood in a silent semi-circle and holding their hands to their mouths, watched their odd visitors with unblinking eyes. An old woman brought a scraggy chicken, thrust it towards me and made as if to cut its throat. Then she took up some rice grains and ran them significantly through her fingers. I took this to mean 'would we care for some chicken and rice for supper?' Seeing how poor they looked I declined and asked instead for some tea. But when the tea was finally brought it was little more than hot water and no more than two or three leaves can have been used in its making. I could only assume that tea was a luxury for them and our simple request had taxed their limited stock. With the watery brew came a ball of solid cheesy substance, streaked with the marks of sooty fingers, pungent and sustaining. The old lady who had brought these provisions was, I suspect, the head man's head wife, for she was privileged to sit with the men round the fire. She squatted there like a gipsy queen, with silver coins sewn into her head scarf, making thread from a handful of black goats' wool by some tricky manipulation of a spinning bobbin.

I had a pair of green plastic sun-glasses, which gave a curious effect when I viewed the flames through them. One of the men took them from me and they were passed from hand to hand amid appropriate gasps of astonishment. Somebody must have been very impressed by them, for I never saw them again and did not like to ask for their return.

Now came the question of where we were going to sleep. It was suggested that Diana join the ladies in one of the round wicker tents, but she thought she would rather sleep in the open. In the end we lay down near the fire on a collection of old rugs; two feet away from my head was a recumbent cow, near my feet a tethered donkey lay, and we went to sleep in deeply breathing animal company.

In the middle of the night this gentle pastorale was disturbed by sounds of violence on the far bank. A lorry had stopped, lights flashed, and blood-curdling Red Indian shouts rang down the valley. I thought that my car was being looted, and that at any minute the camp would be attacked. There was shouting now from our side; a shadowy figure crept towards me, pointed at the far bank, and whispered something in my ear. Was it reassurance or perhaps a warning? Then there was splashing and I told Diana that we were about to be invaded. But it must have been the theatrical backcloth—the jagged rocks, the rushing river, the scudding clouds—that had put all these alarmist ideas into my head, for the two figures who eventually emerged from the flow turned out to be bona fide members of the tribe, delivered by a passing lorry. There must have been many tales to tell, for they chattered on into the small hours around the dying embers a few feet from where we lay.

In spite of their late night, the *kuchis* were up before the sun had appeared over their mountainous confines. Breakfast—hot sweet milk and cheese—was brought to us in bed. Then came the sick parade, when all the women produced their children, mostly wizened little monkeys born of mothers still children themselves, and we had to inspect sores and bad teeth and runny eyes. All we could do was to promise a few pills and powders from our humble pharmacopoeia in the car.

The cows were driven across the river to graze somewhere on the other side. They were clearly experienced, but one or two lost their footing and went swirling down the stream, swimming to shore quite calmly further down. This time Diana mounted the shoulders of a *kuchi* St Christopher and came safely across, to cheers from the other side, with no more than a wetting to her toes.

By afternoon we were down in the sandy foothills, and soon came to Puhl-i-Kumri, a cotton-spinning town, built in the flush of German-influenced industrialization sometime in the late 1930s. There were several large factories surrounded by small white houses for the employees, and a pre-war Berlin-built dam that ran a small hydro-electric plant. In the seedy bazaar that ran through the centre I had the most welcome and delicious drink I have ever had in my life. The old drink-seller had a table beside the *jui* (ditch) set out with bottles containing different coloured syrups. I chose the yellow and the old man produced a glass which, no doubt as a concession to Western ideas of hygiene, he proceeded to wash in a bucket, wiping it dry on his no longer white robes. Then he poured some syrup into the glass and from a piece of sacking produced a lump of very dirty snow. He scraped slivers of snow into the glass which he then filled from the same bucket he had washed the glass in. The resulting mixture, which had a smooth sweet coldness quite different from that produced by ice, was as near nectar as I could imagine and we drank three glasses each before our thirsts were satisfied. This divine drink, locally known as sherbet, was probably deadly with germs for the following day Diana went down with a terrible fever.

Looking round for a rest house or hotel we came upon a promising building, and entering the courtyard saw a notice, CLUB DES AMIS. This smacked of exclusivity and we were about to creep away when a soldier, guarding an inner gate, came over to us.

'Otel?' I asked, and to my surprise he signalled us on through his gate. Within was a well laid-out garden surrounded by buildings. A gaunt young man in khaki shorts at that moment arrived and we began a conversation in German. He was from East Germany and was an engineer at the textile mill; he introduced us to the manager of the 'Club', a friendly Afghan who walked us past a pretty garden of tobacco flowers and lilies to the sleeping quarters.

After we had been installed he produced the Visitors' Book, which I was able to study during his absence in search of a pen. Eighty per cent of the patrons seemed to have been Russians, their names beautifully inscribed in their to-me-incomprehensible script. Some of them were certainly members of 'Techno-Export', responsible for the projected construction at Puhl-i-Kumri of an electricity plant and a cement works. Other guests listed included such interesting and divers characters as Messrs Pesck, Panz and Gorda, (a travelling trio from the Czech Embassy in Kabul); H.E. Ting Koo-Yo; a M. Achour who described himself as 'explorateur'; an author called Edward Hunter; the distinguished French archæologist Schlumberger; and a chorus of 'experts'—'entomologists' (which used once to be synonymous with 'spy'), geologists, engineers, students and assorted technicians—from various Iron Curtain countries.

The northern part of Afghanistan seemed to have been allocated to the Russians as a 'sphere of influence' and often I would see an odd solitary figure walking down a village street, who from the cut of his trousers and the set of his straw hat was unmistakably identifiable as a Soviet Citizen. The most apparent manifestation of Russian activity was the wide road running southwards for over a hundred miles from Mazar-i-Sharif. Beyond Puhl-i-Kumri we met the advancing head of the construction company. A great tented camp lay in a hollow and heavy equipment with Russian markings stood idly by the road. The fashionable colour for their bulldozers and graders seemed to be a royal blue rather than the gaudy orange of Britain and America. The road they were building was wide enough for an army to advance down; though surfaced with grit it was splendidly smooth at first, but as we proceeded northwards, corrugations began to appear. No doubt by the time the end of the road was reached, its beginning, worn out in spite of its width by the ruthless poundings of a steady stream of overloaded lorries, would be as bad as any in Afghanistan, and they would be forced to start the whole process over again. It is probably too expensive to metal them at the same time, but it must be a nightmare to the finance ministry to see enormous sums being spent on the roads and the overall condition steadily deteriorating.

Diana succumbed to the fever at a small town called Tash-Kurgan. It was well down in the plain that extends without a feature into the heart of Russia, hot and stifling, with no relief to body or soul. We stayed there for three terrible days and the only thing I remember with any pleasure was a cherry tree outside the window of the rest house in which a pale turtle-dove sat on her nest of sticks and sobbed a sad *hoo-hoo-hoo* throughout the baking day, her black beady eyes easily confused with the bitter little dark cherries that hung in clusters from the tree.

17

THE NORTHERN ROUTE

MAZAR-I-SHARIF is the main place of pilgrimage in Afghanistan. Its splendid mosque, which houses the tomb of Ali, Fourth Caliph of Islam, is a heavenly building of blue and green tiles. Pure white pigeons flock in its shady forecourts and pattern themselves in flight against its dazzling domes. In spring, when the pilgrimages start, the town is said to be bright with tulips, brought in from the fields around. But that summer, apart from the mosque, Mazar-i-Sharif was a nightmare. The streets were dusty and rutted, lined with filthy ditches. Sordid bazaars hawked the shoddy products of India and Pakistan, cheapjack imitations of standard British goods. Piles of rubble, however, indicated that some great clearance project was in hand.

Diana was barely fit to move, but she thought she might just as well die in the car as in bed and insisted on continuing the journey. I kept her quietly in Mazar for two days and then we set out for the eight-hundred-mile stretch back to Herat.

I had long harboured an ambition to see the Amu Darya, the Oxus of Alexander the Great, Matthew Arnold's 'majestic river' beside which Sohrab and Rustum fought to bloody death. For over seven hundred miles the Amu Darya forms the border between Russia and Afghanistan before it heads northwards across the sands of Kara Kum to end in the Aral Sea. Few people from the West have seen it, for apart from its remoteness it lies in a military area where unsponsored visitors are not encouraged. But I felt I could not call myself a true traveller unless I made at least an effort to see its turgid flow.

A road runs due northwards from Mazar to Termez, where a ferry conveys goods and passengers to and from the Soviet of Uzbekistan. But it soon became clear that it was not just a question of driving there. At the crossroads in Mazar-i-Sharif the only soldier in the whole of Afghanistan who spoke English seemed to have been placed there especially to see that we did not take the northern road.

'Where do you go?' he asked, and I could only reply hopelessly, 'Herat', to be put firmly on the road to the west.

But in fact there was still another chance. Another trade road ran due north through Balkh. Balkh, 'mother of cities', the ancient Bactria, was a place that could reasonably be visited for its touristic interest. Having got there, it might be possible to continue through unchecked.

Fifteen miles beyond Mazar we turned off the main road and without intervention headed northwards towards the ancient town. A saloon car then suddenly appeared behind us, passed, and dropped back, refusing to pass again despite our slow progress. On the outskirts of Balkh we got out to inspect the ancient ramparts of the city. The other car stopped a few yards further on and two men, one in robes and turban, the other in a Western suit, also began a survey of the ruins, though they appeared to be equally interested in us. While they were at the top of a wall that somehow seemed to have escaped Genghiz Khan's destructive fury, we jumped back into the car and quickly drove off before they had time to come down.

I was photographing the ruins of an ancient arch (the Khawaja Akkashe shrine), when another man in a Western suit came up and asked to see my papers. Then a policeman arrived and the two men discussed us in an undertone. There was nothing wrong, apparently, in photographing the ruins of Balkh, for my papers were returned though not with friendliness. With such restrictive supervision I felt it would be wise to return the way I had come. Out of their sight, however, I turned off down a side road, by-passed the town and came out beyond it on the good new road that ran northwards over the featureless steppe as far as the eye could see.

As the sun went down the route became more active. Lorries laden with heavy crates and steel girders from Russia clattered past in clouds of dust; caravans of camels laden with sacks and boxes moved more sedately in the opposite direction. We were now well and truly 'out of bounds'; I began to feel like Hannay in *The Thirty-Nine Steps* that everybody was conspiring to catch me, including the large Russian-built helicopter circling lazily overhead. Somewhere on this plain were said to be secret aerodromes complete with MIGs, but that helicopter, and later a companion, were the only aeroplanes we saw.

Bumping over the dusty stubble round the small town of Khanabad I began to lose heart, picturing exasperated Embassy officials in Kabul working overtime to get us released from the baking local gaol into which we should undoubtedly be thrown 'pending inquiries'. We were now only about ten miles from the river. If we were caught here I should spoil my chances of being allowed to see the minaret . . . then again Diana was ill . . . and the car was going badly—I made every excuse I could think of, but Diana, who seemed to have developed a Death Wish, urged me on. I went on a few miles and then I funked it. I turned across the steppe towards a sandy mound and from this insignificant eminence surveyed the horizon through my glasses. Distantly I saw what I am determined to believe was the reedy marge of Oxus, a green vibrating haze. I also saw what looked like a military vehicle bounding distantly in our direction. I turned round and fled southwards. Darkness was descending and in darkness I felt safe . . .

> But the majestic river floated on,
> Out of the mist and hum of that low land,
> Into the frosty starlight, and there moved,
> Rejoicing, through the hush'd Chorasmian waste,
> Under the solitary moon; he flow'd
> Right for the polar star, past Orgunjé,
> Brimming, and bright and large; then sands begin
> To hem his watery march and dam his streams,
> And split his currents; and for many a league
> The shorn and parcell'd Oxus strains along
> Through beds of sands and matted rushy isles—
> Oxus, forgetting the bright speed he had
> In his high mountain cradle in Pamere,
> A foil'd circuitous wanderer—till at last
> The long'd-for dash of waves is heard, and wide
> His luminous home of waters opens, bright
> And tranquil, from whose floor the new-bathed stars
> Emerge, and shine upon the Aral Sea.

Matthew Arnold's mighty pentameters rolled through my mind. I was glad in a way that the Oxus was denied me in close-up: I believe it is muddy and unattractive in that region. An illusion was preserved and the majestic river floated on, beyond my reach and beyond, for the present, the reach of Martha and her Cadillac.

I should like to state emphatically that in its present condition the road along the northern frontiers of Afghanistan is not to be recommended to travellers, especially in mid-summer. From Mazar to Maimana it ran for four hundred miles across the baking steppe, most of it in such appalling condition that it was necessary to take to the open desert (the home of cousins of our Turkish marmot friends), despite the gullys and patches of scrub that might mean long detours. Miles of the road had given up completely, reduced to deep ruts filled with powdered dust, so that the belly of the car would scrape dangerously on invisible solid objects and the dust follow in a heavy acrid cloud. The thermometer at times topped 125 degrees Fahrenheit, and for four days we ate nothing but cucumbers and melons and drank tea that remained boiling hot all day in its plastic container. Even the nights were hot up there, and it would take several hours for the temperature to drop appreciably after the sun went down.

At night there were the spiders! Or at least the fear of spiders. People in Kabul had warned us against huge yellow-striped tarantulas that patronized that road—great hairy things that would actually spring at you! Deadly poison, too! Or so they said. Diana feared these tales far more than rumours of bandits, and so did I. Driving along at night we could see angry little red eyes reflecting in the headlights. Spiders for sure, though we never stopped to confirm.

It took us two days to reach Andkhoi, little more than 150 miles from Mazar. Here, mercifully, there was a rest house, a square white building perched on the only mound within miles, and happily able to trap an occasional breeze, born perhaps in the distant southern hills, that would creep in at one door, circulate wanly round the passages and then expire. We lay all day on old iron beds, unable to stick a toe outside for the furnace heat. The flies were legion and the water (brought in clusters of little glasses on a wrought-iron stand) was warm and cloudy, but compared with what had gone before this was a life of bliss. In a nearby room a Soviet citizen was listening to popular classics on the wireless—Borodin, Tchaikovsky, and a thundering performance of Rachmaninoff's first Piano Concerto. We saw him in the passage. He wore striped pyjamas and had a close-cropped head and sad Slav eyes. He did not reply to my salute.

We left that hospitable pimple as soon as the sun showed mercy. The road was a little better now and in spite of a delay feasting on water melon at a village *chai-khana* we reached Mai-mana shortly after midnight. I had planned to drive on through and reach the next rest house at Bala-Murghab before the sun became too hot the following day. But we were stopped by policemen who seemed to think this an impossible idea, possibly because we were now only twenty miles from the Russian frontier, and insisted that we stay the night, refusing to return our passports until we agreed.

Thus we had another dehydrating day on the road, though we were now heading southwards with the promise of cool mountains ahead. We found some relief in irrigation ditches watering fields of melon, and revelled in the exquisite pleasure of pouring cans of water over each other. Nor did we hesitate to drink. We would get back into the car with clothes and hair wringing wet, but in a few minutes they would be as dry as a bone again. There was mile after mile of arid sandy foothills before we really began to climb.

Late at night, not far from Kala-Nao, we ran out of petrol. I dared not sleep for fear of missing one of the rare lorries that passed that way. I sat on the bonnet, 'brooding, clasping my knees', dreaming of the sound of distant engines. It must have been about four in the morning when a sudden clatter made me jump up with flapping arms. An ancient lorry, bursting at the seams with passengers, came to a creaking stop.

'What you want?' said a voice surprisingly in English, for a turbaned head was craning from the window of the cab.

'Petrol!' I replied.

'Pet-e-röl? Oh, very good. Where you from? Allemand? Amrika?'

'No. Inglestan,' I said, hoping that this would not disqualify me from assistance.

'Eng-e-land. Oh, very good. Please give driver the value.'

Petrol was siphoned off and gratefully paid for and to echoes of 'Oh, very good!' the phantom lorry disappeared into the darkness.

We were exhausted and could not summon the strength to drive into the town. We slept in the car and limped in next morning with the usual puncture to be mended. I parked Diana in the rest house and set about these routine matters on the edge of the bazaar.

The job was taken on by a lorry driver in a long US army officer's uniform coat. He farmed it out to an eager youth whose keenness to show his speed exceeded his efficiency, for no sooner had he replaced the tyre than it went flat again. I bided my time drinking cup after cup of tea on the veranda of an old *chai-khana*. In front ran a slimy ditch, whose suppurating waters I was almost certainly swallowing. Various local characters in long striped shirts and coloured turbans squatted there with me and did their best to relieve my boredom. As a diversion, when conversation failed, a tame jackdaw called Mia was produced, a charming bird who would hop on to my shoulder and beg grapes. As the bottom half of her beak was broken off her efforts to eat the grapes were ludicrous and she was frequently robbed of her prize by pigeons.

Then, for the second time, the tyre was replaced and for the second time, to the disdainful grunts of the gathering, it subsided with an audible hiss. An ice-cream seller arrived with a tin container surrounded with snow and dirty delicious ices were stood all round. A man with a three-stringed lute drifted up and began to play us a tune. He had two companions with him who, he explained, were members of his band. They did not have their instruments with them and I caused much merriment with my first Afghan-style joke, suggesting that one of them, who was missing three fingers on his right hand, must certainly be the flute player.

The keen but inefficient tyre-fixer now came up and said that the tube was rotten and it was no good trying to mend it any more. I did not immediately despair. The Afghan is an optimist— he assumes that there is never more than one puncture at a time. He will find a hole and mend it; he may listen for a tell-tale hiss from elsewhere but it is against his nature to go through the usual routine of immersing the tube in water and watching for bubbles. This tube seemed perfectly capable of containing air to me.

'Hup! Hup!' I cried, using an invaluable Persian phrase meaning 'OK'. (Persian is the main language of Afghanistan.)

'Hup nist!' came the confident reply and sides were taken on the outcome of the argument. Feeling that the reputation of Western science was at stake I immersed the tube in a puddle and was relieved to discover that there was in fact only one small hole.

When he had mended this and replaced the tyre, all was well. But I had been sitting in that *chai-khana* for about three hours.

The last part of the journey was beautiful and exciting. The road led up through gorges and wooded slopes to a windy upland where stunted cedars grew and eagles flew. These were the classical Paropamisus mountains. We began to descend through valleys flecked with clumps of pampas grass and bright with yellow hollyhocks. Herat, which had become synonymous with home, lay in the plain beyond.

We arrived in darkness and made straight for the friendly 'Park'. Through an open bedroom door an American voice rang out:

'For Chrissake, if you pump that darn thing any more it's going to explode!'

Drinking water was being boiled over a pressure stove. Tins of food and bottles of liquor lay all over the table. We felt superior—hardened travellers who had lived off the land and drunk the water as we found it. 'Water should be boiled for at least twenty minutes, including that for washing the teeth,' said the handout issued by the US Consulate in Kabul. Bearing in mind Diana's fever and the almost continual flux in our insides, I think that perhaps they were right.

18

BEYOND THE MINARET

THE QUESTION of the minaret now had to be faced. It had some-how become the primary objective of a journey I had never really convinced myself was strictly necessary. If I could be the first to stand in the lost city of Firuzkoh I should have raised myself a little way out of the tourist class. But I was unhappy about the whole project: the minaret was a hundred and fifty miles away along the notoriously bad central road, followed by a thirty-mile ride on horses across mountainous country. The northern road had given us a bad pounding; I was tired of driving and the car was tired of being driven—it had no shock absorbers, no hand-brake, no second gear, and was only firing on three cylinders; Diana was as thin as a linnet and not too strong. But she also had the minaret on her mind, and it was her enthusiasm that decided me to go ahead.

The first step was to present Mr Kohzad's letter to the Governor-General. But the Governor-General, it transpired, was away on tour and all my efforts to interest his deputies were un-availing. Then I remembered Amanullah, the English-speaking hotel secretary, and put my problems before him. Amanullah reluctantly undertook to become my *homme d'affaires* at a fee of 100 afghanis per day. He must have been badly in need of money at the time, or I do not think he would have come. He was clearly not cut out for travel in the interior and this, he said, would be the first time he had ever left his wife.

But once committed Amanullah went into action energetically. He borrowed a map from the school (mine had long since been reduced to pulp) and obtained some sort of permit from the Governor-General's office. He was ready to set out the following morning and we picked him up outside his little house at the back of the town. He wore his second best city suit and his habitual *caraculi* hat; a mackintosh was on his arm and he carried delicately before him a pair of smart, light brown shoes which I noticed were made in Japan; a copy of the *Catholic Digest* protruded from his pocket. He had a pick and spade ready, intended, he explained, to clear the road of obstacles rather than for possible archæological excavation on the site of Firuzkoh.

Amanullah felt ill almost from the start. The discomfort of the car was more than he had bargained for, and after a few miles of bumping along the dusty, potholed road his face took on a greenish tinge and he sat hunched up with his head in his hands. Having hired his services as a guide I felt entitled to as much information about the locality as he could provide and ruthlessly questioned him despite his malaise. He did his best, but it was not good enough. 'Amanullah,' I might ask, 'what are those big square buildings with all the holes in the walls?' To which he might reply weakly: 'That is a frequent style of building here,' instead of telling me that they were giant pigeon cotes and that pigeon manure was regarded as being especially good for the cultivation of melons. When I pressed my inquiries further he might reply: 'Mr Alexander. Oy am very sorry. Oy am having trouble with moy stomach.'

The first part of the journey was, in fact, not at all difficult, though the dusty plain of the Hari Rud was whipped by an uncomfortable wind called the Sad-i-bad-i-Bistroz, the 'wind of 120 days', which I had always understood was a traveller's bane, but according to Amanullah was welcomed by the inhabitants of Herat because it made the air a few degrees cooler.

Beyond the small undistinguished town of Obeh we met a limping jeep which contained Max and Mohamet Ali, on their way back to Herat from a scythe-selling trip to Schist. They were feeling very depressed; Max's jeep, a veteran of the war, was giving trouble and they had only managed to dispose of seven scythes.

At Schist Amanullah insisted upon calling on the local governor making use of a field telephone to notify the Governor of Shaharak of our impending arrival. At the time I was against 'officializing' our progress, but in fact Amanullah was doing the correct thing, and I think that without his assistance we should not have got very far towards our objective.

A few miles beyond Schist the road crossed the Hari Rud, at this point a wide and fiercely churning river, by a fine old iron suspension bridge. A board by the side of the road said:

ITISDANGE
ROUSFORLO
ADEDMOTORM
ACHINESTOC
ROSSTHEBR
IDGEPLEAS
EUNLOADBEF
ORECROSSING

We unloaded Amanullah according to these instructions but
Diana insisted on riding across. The floor of loose logs trembled
violently as we crept forwards, but it would have taken more
than a loaded Land Rover to break that old bridge, presumably
British built, and we came safely across.

We now began to enter wilder hillier country—the foothills of
a mountain range. The Hari Rud continued eastwards through its
own deep gorge, casting off our road to loop round to the south.
This country was wild enough and I was suitably alarmed when
rounding a corner we suddenly came upon a man lying in the
middle of the road and three evil-looking Afghans armed with
sickles standing nearby. Were these at last the legendary bandits
I had expected for so long? Amanullah clearly thought so.

'Do not stop! Drive on, please, it is a trick!' he cried
urgently.

'But Amanullah, that man is dead or dying. I must stop. I
cannot just drive on!'

'It is a trap! It is a trap! Drive on or we shall all be
killed!'

But I could not drive on as easily as that, for the body lay
directly across my path. When I stopped, the sinister trio, with
sickles raised, closed in without a word.

'Is he dead?' I asked, pointing to the body.

'He is sick and must be taken to Shaharak!' their spokesman
replied.

'What is the matter with him?' I inquired.

'He has hurt his head!' was the answer.

I was now out of the car and bending over the man; when I
began to prod his head he opened his eyes. He then suddenly sat
up and began to take an interest in the proceedings.

'There is nothing wrong with his head,' I said.

'It is his feet!' cried the men.

I looked at his feet. They were smelly but there did not seem to be anything much wrong with them either.

'There is nothing wrong with his feet!' I said.

'He is tired,' they said. 'He has walked far!'

So Amanullah was right, it was a trick! A simple trick to get a lift for their friend. I was so amused that much to Amanullah's disgust I allowed the now fully activated man to sit on the bonnet. But the road became so bad and his attitude was so ungrateful that I dropped him when we reached some buildings and he limped off with an exaggerated limp and no thank you.

From now on the road was not a road at all, but rather a track made by the removal of larger obstacles from the natural terrain. Sometimes we were running on dried-up river beds and up shallow mountain streams, then there might be a welcome stretch of baked mud or close-cropped turf, or shattering sections where the geological strata ran across like the petrified ribs of some prehistoric monster. These arbitrary conformations climaxed in a chilly 9,000-foot pass whose precipitous corners were difficult to negotiate owing to the mechanical condition of the car. At each corner it was usually necessary to stop, reverse, engage the four-speed, and go ahead again. This was an awkward manoeuvre as the hand-brake did not work and I had to rely entirely on the foot-brake, which meant I really needed three feet. But by using the hand throttle and frantically interchanging limbs it could be managed. Though I did not tell him the worst Amanullah realized there was something wrong for at every corner he took to hopping out, ostensibly to clear the road of obstacles but in fact, as we all knew, to be out of the way should we run backwards or tumble over the edge.

Shaharak lay beyond the mountains and we did not arrive there until ten-thirty, having averaged about ten miles per hour for the journey. If Amanullah had not telephoned I doubt if we should have found it, for there were no more than two stone huts, and had it not been for the waving of hurricane lamps by men who had been sent out to watch for us, we should certainly have driven on past.

The Governor of Shaharak, a charming man with a little 'Hitler moustache', welcomed us with typical Afghan hospitality and feasted us by lamplight on rice and kebab. Amanullah waited

The Governor-General makes a dawn departure

Diana in one of the Governor-General's tents

until we had finished before raising the subject of our coming
with our host.

Thanks to Amanullah's representations and Mr Kohzad's letter
the Governor was prepared to further our trip and to provide
horses and a guide. But when he learned that Diana also was pro-
posing to come, he looked stern and insisted that it was quite out
of the question for a woman to make the trip. The only previous
visitor, the French archæologist Maricq, had come with a Swedish
naturalist and his wife, to whom he had also refused permission.
But Diana, by combining fascination with determination, finally
caused him to withdraw his veto, and in return for my signature
on a document undertaking full responsibility for any untoward
event, included her in the marching orders he then proceeded to
issue.

The next morning, shortly after dawn, our cavalcade was
assembled—Diana in jeans on a flirtatious grey mare, Amanullah
in his mackintosh slumped on a sorry bay, self on a spavined
stallion, and the Governor's aide, turbaned in black and robed in
an outsize US army jacket, on a rival stallion. Two scouts went
on ahead and a third brought up the rear, perhaps to pick up
stragglers.

The minaret, known locally as the Minaret-Jham, lay about
thirty miles across country to the north on the banks of the Hari
Rud. We set off across bare brown hills, our horses picking their
practised way along the steep and stony tracks. From the marks in
the dust it looked as if a versatile motor-bike had already passed
that way, but it was only the footprints of the guides, whose
home-made leather shoes were soled with sections of motor tyre.
The sun shone fiercely but the mountain air was cool. Enormous
eagles wheeled high above us, black butterflies hovered over the
turf as if they were cropping it; sometimes I spotted a horned wild
sheep eyeing us from a distant ridge. Wherever there was water
there was likely to be an encampment of *kuchis*, whose sinister
black tents were guarded by dogs, full of sound and fury but shy
of a well-aimed stone. We lunched at one of their camps on a
greasy plateau, sucking runny boiled eggs in the approved Afghan
fashion and scooping up yoghourt with bread.

Amanullah, the city man, had a very feudal approach to the
kuchis. He always seemed to be shouting roughly at them.
'*Injah!*' he would bark, meaning 'come here!' When I gently

chided him he said huffily, 'Mister Alexander. Oy know moy people. They are very disobedient!' But by the time the journey was over he had developed a more sympathetic approach to the nomads of the hills, and once said confidentially that he would not mind having a *kuchi* wife himself.

They stood round watching us with interest, especially Diana, who was probably the first European woman they had ever seen. She made friends with a young woman who was sitting over an iron pot watching the water boil. In the water were some twigs, the local equivalent of a detergent ('These are mountain people. These are simple people,' said Amanullah apologetically as if to explain the absence of OMO). According to Amanullah's translation this woman said of Diana: 'No wonder she looks so happy! She is roaming round the world. And I just sit here washing!' Diana explained that she did her own washing at home, and sat down beside the woman and helped her wring the clothes. They were soon good friends and before we left the woman said to Amanullah, 'I like her very much. If she was a Moslem I should like her to stay here.' The men had less religious discrimination and I turned down several offers of sheep and cows in exchange.

There was the usual sick parade, with women thrusting forwards their sore-covered children and pathetically baring their own rotting gums for inspection. Amanullah seemed to resent this revelation of their ailments as if it reflected unfavourably on the medical service of his country. The main cause of all the trouble seemed to be vitamin deficiency: vegetables, apparently, form no part of the *kuchi* diet, and will not grow at these heights. It is surprising they have evolved no substitute.

We rode on again and as the sun went down we came to the stone hut which was to be our shelter for the night. We were greeted by a bearded patriarch with a local reputation for holiness. He wore a long padded coat over his robes with one enormously long sleeve that hung down like a broken wing. He was attended by an acolyte (his grandson), a lank-locked young man with a delinquent eye. Other bearded tribesmen assembled and we were feasted on the skewered liver of a baby goat that had been killed in our honour. But we were so tired and stiff that we rudely fell asleep, almost in mid-meal, among the rugs and cushions on the floor.

Next morning I was fretting to make an early start. The

Governor wanted his horses back by the following evening, so that we only had one day to reach the minaret and return to the hut. It seemed an age before they were finally saddled up, and I began to feel like M. Maricq that I should not have time to see the ruins that lay beyond the minaret.

There were many more khaki-coloured ridges to cross before we descended a steep slope into a verdant valley. Negotiating the slippery path Amanullah fell off his horse. 'Oy think oy have broken moy head!' he moaned, and thereafter took to walking in the more difficult places.

A clear and pleasant stream ran along the valley. We followed the mint-fringed watercourse through fields of sweet-smelling grass, weaving among groves of poplar and orchards of apricot, which we plucked and ate, sun-warmed, as we rode. I took this stream to be the Hari Rud and expected the minaret to come into view at any minute, riding on ahead with the childish aspiration of being the first in our party to see it. But by midday there was still no sign of it. Two hours later the valley narrowed and became bare and rocky. Rounding a bend we suddenly saw it, a colossal tower rearing up at the end of a narrow defile about a hundred yards ahead. This sudden confrontation quite took away what little breath I had left.

It was a formidable, at the same time elegant, object, standing its ground as arrogantly as a missile on a launching-pad—two hundred odd feet of honey-coloured brick soaring skywards in three cylindrical stages. It was no ruin, but a major monument, and its isolated presence among those lonely monotonous hills affected us with a sense of pure surprise. The Afghan attendants gasped with us.

The whole shaft was elaborately decorated in high relief brickwork. The lower stage, rising from an octagonal base, was composed of honeycomb panels bordered with a text in Kufic script that by the time it had scissored to its tortuous conclusion had spelt out the entire nineteenth sura of the Koran, over a thousand words. The second stage, separated by the rotting timbers of the gallery or *guldest*, announced in a circlet of blue *faience* the name and titles of its builders: 'The magnificent sultan, the august King of Kings Ghiyath ud-Din Abu'l Fath,[1] glorifier of Islam and the faithful companion of the Emir of the Faithful'. Above was the

[1] Died at Herat in A.D. 1220.

Moslem declaration of faith: 'There is no God but Allah, and Mohamet is the prophet of Allah.'

The men tethered the horses around the massive base, the circumference of which was about ninety feet, and began to prepare a meal. Amanullah, still suffering from his fall, rolled up in a rug and went to sleep. Diana and I went to bathe in a turquoise pool that glinted through the bushes. This pool turned out to be a wide stretch of river, in fact the Hari Rud—the stream we had so long followed was its tributary, the Jham. The minaret stood in the right angle formed at the confluence of these two rivers. Above the pool were the remains of a brick-built bridge. Beyond, atop a high spur, I could make out the crumbling battlements of a ruined city.

After a swim I climbed the minaret, squeezing in through a narrow aperture about ten feet from the ground. The walls at this point were over seven feet thick and constructed of flat, fired bricks, about eight inches square and two inches high. I climbed the spiral staircase for about 150 feet until they ended at a platform of brick bound by iron-hard plaster. I was able to pass through this shelf and to climb up little stairs projecting from the drum through a succession of five vaulted platforms. Only the last fifteen feet to the top were impossible to climb for there were no supports, the wooden beams had rotted, and the blue sky showed through the top of the lantern tower.

Descending to what I took to be my point of entry I was surprised to find that the ground lay twice as far below and that the window was too narrow to pass through. As there was no exit further down I was puzzled and even alarmed by the mystery. I was forced to retrace my steps to the top before I solved the problem: there were two apertures in the landing and two separate spiral staircases leading down the bottom section of the shaft. This was utterly unexpected and I believe is unique in the construction of minarets. It seemed to have escaped M. Maricq's notice.

An old man, owner of a nearby apricot orchard, who had trailed along behind us, told me that there had been a tunnel running from the tower under the river. Such legends are usual with old buildings, but this might well have been true, for I found cellars blocked with rubble. The absence of an entry other than the window I had climbed through further supported the theory.

The location of Firuzkoh, summer capital of the Ghori kings, has long puzzled historians. The thirteenth-century chronicler Abu 'Umr-i-Usman refers several times to the 'river of Firuzkoh'. Ravery, his nineteenth-century translator, suggests in a footnote that this was probably 'a feeder of the Hari Rud, if not the main stream, which rises in Ghor', but Sir Thomas Holdich, Chief of the Russo–Afghan Boundary Commission, who travelled in that part of the country in 1884–85, could find no trace of it, and held that it was situated at Taiwara on the Farah River to the south, which is still known locally as Ghor. Others held that it lay by the Upper Murghab River to the north.

Certainly what I saw seemed to bear out Mr Kohzad's theory that Firuzkoh was directly related to the minaret. On the river bank opposite my point of crossing (I was forced to leave my camera behind owing to the strength of the current) I came upon the ruins of what might once have been a building with a circular dome. This could have been the *Jami Masjid*, or 'collecting mosque', which is described in the chronicle[1] as having been 'destroyed by a flood'.

I scrambled up rocks and a steep bank of scree and reached what seemed to be a series of five towers and connecting walls following the contours of the hill. This may well have been the *kasr* or citadel of Firuzkoh, described as being 'an edifice the like of what is not found in any country or in any capital—a kasr . . . with buttresses, balconies and tunnels, and of such configuration as no geometrician has made manifest. Over that kasr are placed five pinnacles inlaid with gold, each of them three ells and a little over in height and in breadth two ells, and also two gold *tumae*[2] each about the size of a large camel. . . .'

The town itself, identifiable by rudimentary foundations and piles of stones, extended about half a mile into the hills behind. A large water cistern, well-built sewers, and the foundations of an arched bridge over the river, gave evidence of an effective civilization. I picked up various pieces of attractively glazed pottery of pre-Mongol period—the base of a bowl glazed inside over a white slip with green spots; part of a slipware jug elegantly decorated with a thick black brushline; part of a bowl decorated with sgraffito; and a piece with a red burnish of an earlier date.

[1] The Tabakat-i-Nasiri of Abu 'Umr-i-Usman.
[2] A mythical bird.

This must once have been a place of power and beauty: I was almost certainly standing in Firuzkoh, ancient capital of the mountain kings whose court was 'graced with learned doctors of religion and law ecclesiastical, accomplished scholars, illustrious philosophers and the celebrated in eloquence . . . the asylum of the world and the retreat of the worthy and laudable persons of the earth.'

I was filled with the desire to uncover the secrets of this mysterious isolated city. But across the river Amanullah, in one of his masterful moods, was excitedly signalling for me to return. If we did not start immediately we should not reach the stone hut that night. As it was, in spite of taking a difficult short cut over a mountain, we nearly lost it in the descending darkness.

We were offered a choice of two routes back from the stone hut— the one by which we had come, or an easier and more beautiful one, though longer. I chose the second and the extra length was justified by a long wide valley, green with corn and poplars and dotted with ghostly villages made of mud which had been completely deserted while their inhabitants camped with their sheep and cattle on the upper slopes.

Once we met a band of horsemen who galloped towards us each with an arm in the air and reined up within a few yards like cowboys. They were only showing off and continued laughing on their way. But most of the people we met were travelling more sedately on the backs of cows.

This halcyon valley finally petered out in a sandy plain; distantly visible across a stream was a busy scene of men and horses, and tents in the process of being erected. I rode over to investigate and the first person I saw was our old friend the governor of Shaharak. The reason for all the excitement, he explained, was the imminent arrival of the Governor-General of Herat, who was touring the country and had arrived at Shaharak *en route* to inspect the minaret which we had just left. This camp had been prepared for his reception and here he intended to stay the night. The Governor of Shaharak offered us tea and said that if we liked to wait a little we could meet the Governor-General.

We were sitting down sipping tea in an enormous Peshawar-made tent painted with pink roses when a big figure strode in. He was wearing a peaked American canvas cap, dark glasses, a belted canvas jacket, brown riding breeches and brown suede boots. He had a beaked nose and humorous eyes and looked every inch a Governor-General, or even a Roman emperor. He shook hands with us and invited us to sit beside him on his special rug. By now the tent was filling with bearded turbaned tribesmen who had come to pay their respects. Amanullah sat opposite, very deferential, with his legs crossed and every now and then rising to his feet to make a little speech. The Governor-General seemed very off-hand with the old chiefs who were sitting all around, hardly giving them a word and addressing all his attentions to Diana, who was seated by his side. A woman, unveiled, at the Governor-General's side, must have given them cause for many headshakings when they returned to their tents.

After the audience some of the men dispersed, but the more important ones remained for a feast that was now laid before us. It was Diana's twenty-first birthday and it looked as if she was going to be able to celebrate it in an appropriate fashion after all. It was a splendid banquet and I can remember eating consecutive mouthfuls of liver, fried fish, sheep's tail, yoghourt, mutton, marrow, melon, curry and apricot jam.

In between mouthfuls we chatted to the Governor-General about his tour. He had been on the move for the past three weeks and had travelled hundreds of miles through his province, which I gather is not the usual practice of Afghan Governor-Generals. I asked him about the great gatherings of the *kuchis* that I had heard assembled in the upper valley of the Hari Rud. He had been there recently and he described the great grassy plain and the rows of tents and stalls where all the products of Asia were displayed for sale. Most of the *kuchis*, the governor said, were armed, and there were rifles enough to equip a division. 'Are you soldiers or merchants?' he had been constrained to ask, and at his departure they had all fired salvoes in the air.

The Governor-General was interested to hear of our experiences at Bamyan. 'How were my trees doing?' he asked. He was referring to the splendid avenues of poplar he had caused to be planted when that part came under his governorship. 'I was a young man, then,' he said with a sigh, 'and full of enthusiasm.' The job he would really like, he said, was to be ambassador to England. I am sure that London would love the Governor-General and I hope that one day we shall welcome him there.

He was tired after his journey and so were we. Added to which he planned to be on his way at dawn. The Governor of Shaharak, who had been fussing in the background with the responsibility for all the organization on his mind, showed us to a pretty circular tent. Here, guarded by a soldier without, Diana and I and Amanullah spent the night. It was very cold and in the early morning I was aware of the shadowy form of Amanullah gently putting one of his blankets over me.

The Governor-General's party was up at dawn as advertised and even as the sun rose there was a stamping and a neighing of horses being saddled. The sun came up with great speed and before long it was just another hot day. After breakfast and good-byes, the Governor-General, his entourage, and a large amount of baggage including a case of shotguns, moved off towards the minaret. As he disappeared into the distance I realized that the film I had given him as a present was a super-fast one. I hope his photographs were not all over-exposed.

The Governor-General lent us his YAK, a Russian jeep-like vehicle, to take us back to Shaharak. This was a relief, for a long ride on an extraordinarily uncomfortable nail-studded Afghan saddle had made me stiff and sore.

In our condition of physical discomfort the drive from Shaharak to Herat was a great strain. The tyres of the Land Rover were in a state of disintegration and on two of them small rubber balloons extruded from slits in the outer casing with only a protective piece of folded inner tube between us and an explosion. Every so often I would get out to see how thin the rubber was wearing. It lasted a surprising number of miles before it became necessary to insert a new piece.

We stopped for lunch with the Governor at Schisht. It was Friday and he was at ease in his pyjamas. We joined him in an enormous plate of curried mutton. The flies were so bad that Diana, who has a horror of insects, had to get up and leave the room; later I found her outside changing the wheel, a job she insisted on attempting all by herself, I think, in order to demonstrate to Amanullah that women were at least as good as men.

Leaving her to it, I walked up with Amanullah to look at the ruined mosque on the hill, which dated from Ghori days. From the top of a piny eminence there was a view over the leafy valley, green from the springs of Schisht. Beyond the mosque was a

more modern tomb built by a former Governor-General of Herat
to honour some holy man whose name I have forgotten. The holy
man was an ancestor of Amanullah's wife so he had a special
interest in the place and went into the tomb to say his prayers.
I was made to wait outside.

I asked Amanullah why it was that the Afghans were so serious
about their religion, when they seemed such a free and easy
people. 'Mister Alexander,' he replied gravely, 'when an Afghan
loves something, he loves it completely. Loving his religion is
for him like loving a woman.' Amanullah, who obviously held
some of the reformist views of his namesake king, was prepared
to admit that there was scope for modification in the Afghan
interpretation of the Prophet's teachings, especially as regards
women, and he thought they might be freed from the veil within
the next ten years. He was critical, too, of some of the shibboleths.
'What is the meaning exactly of that hand drawn on the wall?' I
asked. Outlines of hands were frequently to be seen traced on
buildings and I knew that they had something to do with the
Evil Eye! But Amanullah was not forthcoming. 'It is nothing,'
he insisted. 'Just a superstition. It is only for very simple people.'
'And why do they have those tattered banners flying over their
graves?' Amanullah might have described the charming custom
whereby the friends and relatives of the departed fly a flag to show
he is not forgotten. But he would not be drawn out and would
only say: 'They are very stupid people.'

Amanullah then had a question for me.

'Mister Alexander.'

'Yes, Amanullah.'

'Mister Alexander, in the Christian religion, if a man has intercourse with a woman is it laid down that he should wash before
and after? This is the second most important rule of the Moslem
religion.'

I could only reply that it was a point of hygiene rather than
dogma, adding what seemed to be a pertinent question for certain
parts of Afghanistan: 'What happens if there is no water?'

'Then they are excused,' said Amanullah gravely.

Diana, hot, dusty and oily, had vindicated her sex by changing
the wheel. Amanullah did his best not to look impressed. Then
we said good-bye to the Governor of Schisht and rattled off again.

We came to Obeh in the early evening. Amanullah, anxious to

6

prolong the trip and his salary as a cicerone for as long as possible, said that a few miles up in the hills to the north were some famous sulphur springs. There was a hotel there. We could take a bath and spend the night.

We followed a tree-lined gully up into the hills. A blue and steaming stream danced beside us. After about five miles we came to the baths. It was dusk and the attendants were surprised to see anybody at that hour. But they girded up their robes and I followed into a small tiled room at the end of which was a deep rectangular bath. There was no trouble about taps: water of perfect temperature flowed straight from the stream through a conduit in the wall and out again through the bottom of the continually replenished bath. I lay there in the half-light in a dream of bliss; the aches in my bones eased out and I felt my sun-flaked skin becoming soft and smooth again. I basked in this fountain of youth for over an hour.

Amanullah went to sleep in his bath and we were installed in the hotel by the time he arrived. We, too, were tugged by sleep and had surrendered to it before a meal could be brought.

19

HERAT II

I LEARNED over a dish of mulberries at the Iranian Consulate (the only foreign representation in Herat) that there had been a *coup d'état* in Iraq and that Nuri Saad had been killed. This came as a great surprise and I remembered the words of the Britisher I met in Teheran, brash and in bad taste:

'We've got the place sewn up. They're paying the money and we're playing the tune. They're in the bag all the time though they don't know it. . . . If we weren't there they'd just squat around in the sun and go to sleep!' It was that sort of attitude, I reflected, that lost allies as well as empire.

In spite of the sad news, soon amplified with details of King Feisal's murder, there was a merry party in progress at the Park. Some Americans were in the room next door and insisted that we join them for a drink. There were only three of them though it sounded like a dozen: a gentle, elderly man with pepper and salt short hair called Jim; a vocal but friendly man who I came to know as 'Boise', because he came from Boise, Idaho; and the most American of the lot in a loud Florida shirt and accent to match, who turned out to be a pure Afghan called Khalil. The trio were employed in an organization called CAAG which was concerned in the building of aerodromes.

Khalil was quite a character. With some good English gin inside him he came out with some extraordinarily funny stories about his time in England, where he had studied for seven years with EMI. I wish he would publish them if only to make the point that the customs of the natives of that country are far more peculiar than in any of the places written up by her roving sons. In particular I enjoyed his description of a hopeless meeting with an incomprehensible Yorkshire girl in Hyde Park complete with imitation of her accent; then there was a fantastic scene in Walham Green when he was ducked and almost drowned in the public baths; a week-end at Butlins, Bournemouth (much enjoyed); and a meeting with an 'existentialist' girl called Dorothy, who introduced him to some of the King's Road 'Angries'. The originality of Dorothy's décor and the nihilistic opinions of her friends had left its mark on Khalil and something of their thought processes was amusingly revealed when Jim started asking keen questions about local history. . . .

'This guy Genghiz Khan. When did he live?'

Khalil passionately put forward the theory that it was not dates that mattered but the spiritual motivations behind the dates.

'History is people, not dates,' he insisted. Jim was not having any of this:

'Christopher Columbus discovered America in 1492. If that isn't history I'd like to know what is.' The argument warmed up a little.

'Of course, that's the trouble with you Afghans . . .' Jim began to say, when he felt he might be going a little too far and fell back on one of his favourite prefaces. 'My wife and I. . . .' This time he sensitively but quite unnecessarily, for Khalil was a great deal more sophisticated than he was, tried to make amends by stating:

'My wife and I have had the best welcome in Afghanistan than in any country we've been in . . .'

Viewed from the Afghan standpoint Khalil was something of a renegade. I asked Mohamet Ali to come and join the party but he refused. He said he was tired, and so too, was Max. I know for a fact that they both disapproved.

There were occasional glimpses in the corridor of girls. And though 'Boise' gave them a hail they were not feeling sociable either. It was not until the following morning that they were revealed as two German girls travelling in company with a Pakistani gentleman. Their destination, as was obvious from the large painted sign above the roof of the Pakistani's big American car, was OSLO: their provenance PESHAWAR. This car was to be in our company half-way across Persia and the 'Pakistani gentleman' was to become our good friend Mr Shah, and the 'two German girls' Walburga and Miss Thiel respectively.

Mr Shah was agent for General Motors in Peshawar. He was also, as I noted on his passport, a *Sayyed* or descendant of the Prophet and when I asked him if he could do better than the gentleman in Meshed, who had claimed to be the twenty-sixth in line, he produced a crumpled genealogical tree from his pocket, which put him somewhere down among the late thirties.

The front of Mr Shah's car was decked with the metal badges of innumerable motoring clubs.

'There are many more in his office,' said Walburga, who seemed to have a secretarial job in Mr Shah's (she called him 'Shah Sahib') office. I never quite discovered why they were going to Oslo together, nor could I make out the role of Miss Thiel (she was always called 'Miss Thiel', though a peep in her passport told me that her name was Wilhelmina). It seemed that she had taken a job in a Peshawar kindergarten; her boy friend was now thought to want to marry her and she was returning to Hamburg with her fingers crossed all the way. Miss Thiel was anxious, bossy and rather touchy. She was pale and washed-out by the heat of the plains, not as pretty as Walburga, a buxom girl with a fringe, but the more we got to know her the more we liked her.

We arranged to travel in convoy to Teheran, a plan which suited me well as the car was reeling from the rough treatment it had been subjected to on the trip to the minaret. They left Herat a little before us but we caught them up an hour or two later near the *caravanserai* where we had been so needlessly scared on our way in. They certainly had no fear of bandits: they were eating their supper in the middle of the road by the glare of their car's headlights. We gratefully shared their last course, eaten off smart plastic plates from a picnic basket, of cheese and 'Buchanan's Cream Crackers', delicious biscuits made in Pakistan, one of the more lasting legacies of the British (Scottish) Raj to Indian civilization.

We travelled to the frontier together. At the suggestion of two gentlemen in dove-grey robes and blonde caraculi hats we stayed the night in the guest-house on the Afghan side, deferring frontier formalities until the following morning.

The aged roadman was still treading his purgatorial path across the stony no-man's-land. At the Persian frontier they had a message for us from Tony to say that he had passed that way and that his bicycle was going well. In the next town, while filling up with petrol and Coca-Cola, I heard a voice saying 'Iskandar! Iskandar!' and I turned to see the gendarme who had given us his hospitality on the way through.

'Shikar? Shikar?' he said and shook his head, laughing. And

then at Meshed, waiting for a tyre to be repaired, who should come up on a bicycle but the gendarme's young brother. He was very pleased to see us, in particular Diana, with whom he had undoubtedly fallen in love. He came to lunch at our hotel laden with fruit and sweetmeats, and confessed that he had stolen her photograph on our first meeting, which he now wished to return as it had been on his conscience. No doubt he had proudly passed it round to all his friends at Meshed University.

Diana still nursed her ambition to see inside the great Meshed mosque, strictly forbidden ground where very few 'unbelievers' have trod. She asked her young man if he would take her there, and such was his infatuation that he agreed. After lunch he went off to his sister's house and returned with the regulation black ground-length *chador* or veil, and a pair of thick lisle stockings. We rigged her out in the bedroom and with her sunburned skin and dark eyes she looked convincingly of the country. If challenged she would say she was 'Hindi', a lady from India.

I, of course, was not included in the arrangements, and it was with some anxiety that from the hotel window I saw her black veiled figure slipping down the street on her way to the shrine of shrines, for this was the period of *Moharram* when the Shi'ites mourn the martyrdom of Messrs Ali, Hussein and Hassan, those unfortunate claimants to the mantle of Mohamet murdered by the rival protagonists, the Sunnites, who form the majority of the Islamic world. I had read of orgies of fanaticism that took place with scourgings and screamings and self-mutilations and a very unhealthy atmosphere in general. I was only partly reassured by Diana's escort telling me that this was only the beginning of *Moharram* and that the real fun did not begin for another ten days.

While the two pilgrims were away I wandered out into the street and did a little market research on the subject of bicycles, of which there seemed to be almost as many in Meshed as there are motor-scooters in Milan. Two-barred models were *de rigueur*, with smart plastic saddle covers and decorated with silken bobbles of red and green (the Iranian national colours). Almost every bicycle was of British manufacture, in particular Phillips and Hercules. I was examining one of these makes outside a shop when its young Iranian owner came up and pointing at his mount said proudly, 'Amrikan. Amrikan.' I think he must have confused Birmingham, Warwickshire, with Birmingham, Alabama, and he looked very disappointed when I assured him that it had in fact been 'Made in England'.

The Russians were carrying out an assault on this market and there were advertisements in the local papers saying 'Soviet Satellites in the Sky—Soviet Bicycles on the Ground'. The Russian model, offered like all Russian exports to Iran on generous credit terms, was selling for 2,500 rials complete, whereas the Hercules was 2,800 rials less accessories. Russia was only forty miles away to the north and a continual stream of goods could be seen coming in from the Bajgiram–Ashkabad frontier. But, said a local dealer, spinning round the wheel of a Russian model, he did not think much of it: the ball bearings were no good, and it only had one bar.

Diana returned about an hour later looking pleased with herself. She could now call herself *Meshedi*, having seen the tomb of the great Imam Reza. She had found frantic pilgrims climbing up and down the bars of the shrine and had felt that she was expected to do the same. But her main embarrassment had been when her lisle stockings kept falling down and she had an anxious moment when one of the guardians came angrily up to her and ordered her to pull her veil further over her brow.

Mr Shah and the girls stayed in our hotel. On our last afternoon in Meshed the Pakistan Consul took us all to a pleasant park in the town and we ate ice-creams on the terrace in front of a boating lake, upon which a Persian family was leisurely rowing, Shah Reza must have had a hand in planning the place for there were the familiar silver nymphs and lions and urns.

The Shah party had an invitation to dinner in Meshed. As we did not wish to spend another night there, we left them in the park and set off in the evening towards Teheran, arranging to meet them for breakfast somewhere along the road. We did not plan to take the northern road through Bujnurd, but instead to follow the conventional route running due west across the plains.

Our journey started badly enough when one of the second-hand Japanese tyres I had just bought exploded with a bang and nearly had us in the ditch. A passing motorist came to our rescue and sold me an old inner tube at twice its value and we patched the tyre up as best we could.

About twenty miles out of the town we met a long convoy of lorries. The leading jeep signalled us to stop and an officer got out and came over to us.

'You must go back! You must go back!' he cried. 'Back to Meshed!' I turned round and made as if to conform. But instead of returning to Meshed I turned off the road at the first opportunity, parked the car behind a bank of sand and turned off the lights. Soon the lorries began to roar past us and were gone. Then came a new noise: a clattering, clanking sound, and I began to make out sinister silhouettes in the gloom. They were cruiser tanks of American manufacture. Twenty of them rolled by, at intervals of thirty yards. A shadowy figure stood in the cockpit of each. Then all was silent.

Where were they going to? Were they off to the railhead and thence to Baghdad to quell the rebels? Or to the Russian frontier as an insurance against the Russian troop movements that were said to be taking place? With such speculations in our heads we pulled further out into the desert and went to sleep.

Continuing early next morning we passed several tanks that had fallen by the wayside.

'Baghdad?' we shouted as we passed. And they smiled and gave us a version of the 'thumbs-up' sign.

Mr Shah caught up with us as we changed a wheel. The car was behaving badly and it was a relief to have their escort in case of serious trouble. The road to Teheran was in need of a new surface. Heavy transport had reduced it to series of washboard corrugations, only tolerable if one attained maximum speed and skimmed along the top. The great lorries[1] acted on this principle and roared along at fifty miles an hour and more. It was essential to get out of their Juggernaut way, for they never swerved from their dead central course for a smaller car and it is likely that if they had done so their wheels would have wavered and landed them in the ditch. Judging by the carcasses that lined the road this was a frequent occurrence. I never really appreciated until then the dramatic intensity inherent in Clouzot's film, *The Wages of Fear*, when the driver of a lorry laden with high explosive is

[1] Most of the lorries were American or German. British lorries had the reputation of being unable to stand up to the poundings. A further criticism was that most British lorries had the driver's cabin over the front axle, which has a disintegrating effect even on the strongest spine.

*rthcoming attraction,
shed*

*eaking off to the
osque, Meshed: Diana
guised as a Moslem*

'Diana of the Uplands', Paropamisus Mountains

faced with the problem of whether to take the corrugations slow or fast.

We had a few diversions on that grinding three-day trip—a routine visit to Omar Khayyàm's pretty tomb near Nishapur, picnics in shady orchards, and sleeping by the roadside. At supper one night the largest scorpion I have ever seen appeared on Mr Shah's tablecloth, which caused his party to sleep in the car instead of beside it, a position we had long adopted for safety.

With water spurting from a broken pump, two cylinders only firing, the body coming apart from the chassis and all the tyres (one Russian, one Japanese, one Dutch, one Dunlop) in shreds, we limped the last fifty miles to Teheran in a burning sandstorm. Even Mr Shah's big car was beaten up. He broke two springs and had a repair bill of over £50.

EVERYBODY in Teheran was talking about the landings in Lebanon and Jordan and the Iraq *coup d'état*. Three bearded sheikhs, in whiter than white robes, were huddled conspiratorially in the ante-room of the Hotel Caravan; in our old 'Baudelaire' a dark gentleman in the room next door said to me proudly, apropos of nothing for I had not addressed him, 'I am Arab from Kuwait. I do not speak English.' At lunch with the Air Attaché I met an official of Skyways Airline who had just arrived from Beirut. He had actually watched the Americans landing and graphically described the performance.

'I've never seen anything like it,' he said. 'They didn't look human. Like Martians. Those space helmets and fierce expressions and all hung with bombs and some weapons I'd never set eyes on before . . . Atomic disintegrator ray-guns, I expect.'

The Air Attaché, Pelly-Fry, had been down to the Iraq frontier in his aeroplane (shared with his opposite number in Ankara) to rescue evacuating British citizens. He had been disappointed not to find any, a situation that had not prevented the British Press from billing him as 'The Scarlet Pimpernel of the Middle East'. Michael Gillam, the frogman from the Caspian, had also been there. A border policeman who remembered the oil crisis had said to him pithily:

'You British always make trouble for yourselves. First you evacuate everybody from Iran to Iraq, now you evacuate them all back again. It would be much simpler if you stayed at home.'

In Teheran the Consul had laid on a great emergency operation to provide accommodation for the expected refugees, and British residents had a recrudescence of the Dunkirk spirit, rallying round with camp beds and extra blankets. But all to no avail for no more than half a dozen people came that way.

Most Iranians seemed very disturbed by events in Iraq. Not being in any way related to the Arabs they had no interest in Arab nationalism, and their security was compromised by the defection of a member of the Baghdad Pact. But the Persian

'Radical Set', among whom I had some acquaintances, were of the opinion that there was virtue in the revolution. It had been touch and go in Iran also, they said, and the Shah's palace had been ringed with tanks in case of trouble. But I never found confirmation of this.

We saw a lot of Leli at that time. Her parents had a big house with a beautiful swimming pool and we spent several pleasant afternoons lying on the green lawn that surrounded it, drinking iced water-melon juice with her brothers and friends. Shireen said:

'It must have been like this on the eve of the Russian revolution.' Shireen was studying Sociology at London University, and was off to spend the summer working in a village with an American research team. She was a beautiful girl, with a strong will and determined personality. Her father had been governor of a Caspian province and she was completely reversing the traditional system whereby the daughters of smart families stay at home or are seen at parties and are not encouraged to take an interest in the common people. I think it is true to say that a social sense is not inherent in the Persian personality, everything I have read on the subject and everything I saw suggested that self-interest and personal gain and advancement lay at the bottom of all their actions. But there were signs of a change of heart and the deluge may be diverted by appreciation of the fact that even self-interest may necessitate an acceptance of social responsibilities.

Leli's grandfather was Doctor Mossadegh and the impression I gathered of the old man, who was at that time living in retirement in the country, was that he was not just 'that long-nosed little trouble-maker in pyjamas', as I heard him described in British circles in Teheran, but a radical reformer righteously indignant at the way things were being run. His family, at any rate, seemed to believe the stories about the unhappy activities of the oil interests and Leli's brother told me in all seriousness that after the takeover a secret pipeline running into Iraq used to avoid paying royalties to the Persians had been discovered. Apart from arrogance and exclusivity the main charge against the British oil interests, he said, was meanness, an opinion that was echoed in the vernacular by a gentleman I met in the Teheran Club, which I quote verbatim:

'A chap goes out to some God-forsaken spot where the local big chief is sitting on a gold-mine; he doesn't know what to do with it. You've got the knowhow and you'll take the gamble. So you offer him a string of beads for it and he goes away as happy as hell with the string of beads round his neck. In twenty years' time when the mines or the wells or the whathaveyous are coughing up the whatnots, along comes the old chief and says, "Look, all I've got is a string of beads" . . . Well, it's either out with the knobkerries or you say, "Let's have a parley." And you end by giving him another string of beads to keep him happy. No sense in being unreasonable! Trouble with the oil boys, they were too mean with the beads. . . .'

Just before we were due to leave Teheran I became involved in a situation that might well have delayed our departure for several days.

At seven in the morning the hotel porter burst into my room and told me that I was wanted downstairs by the police. I found two of them in the hall talking to the manager. In the background was the boy whose job it was to keep an eye on the car in the street outside; from the hangdog expression on his face I could only assume that it had been stolen. Then I realized that there was another reason for their visit: one of the policemen was carrying my Luger automatic.

Throughout the journey the pistol had reposed safely wrapped up in rags in the toolbox under the seat. He must have unearthed it while cleaning the car. Every hotel had its informer: I wondered if the boy had betrayed me to the police, or if he had merely been playing with it and they had seen it. His behaviour suggested the first alternative, for he would not look me in the eye and seemed to be on familiar terms with the policemen.

On the face of it it was quite a serious situation. The Persians were sensitive about arms. I had not declared mine at the frontier nor had I obtained a permit. Before I went off to the police station I asked Mr Shah to make inquiries on my behalf if I did not return to the hotel within three hours.

At the local station booted gendarmes inspected me in a not unfriendly way and passed the offending weapon from hand to hand comparing it with the smaller sidearms they carried themselves. An interpreter was found in the shape of a worried young

Arab who had come to the station to report the loss from his
hotel bedroom of his entire possessions, passport and money
included. A bulldog major now arrived and everybody leaped to
their feet and stood to attention. I expected the worst when he
started barking staccato questions, but when I explained that I had
brought the pistol strictly for use in Afghanistan against dogs and
possibly bandits, he seemed to relax; he was quite willing to think
of the Afghans as a race of wild men and agreed that it was
reasonable enough to want to take a pistol *there*. But the law was
the law and there were certain due processes to be gone through.
As I was in the wrong I did not protest and at the end of the
questioning the major, according to the interpreter, made a little
speech to his men pointing out what nice people the English
were, at heart. I wondered whether this was a spontaneous
tribute, or another manifestation of an official policy to improve
the climate of popular opinion towards the West.

The major insisted that I get in touch with the British Consul.
Much against my will, considering the ignominy of the incident
and the fact that it was a Saturday, I telephoned the Consul and
he appeared shortly afterwards without seeming unduly annoyed.
Then began a round of visits to various offices, looking for an
appropriate authority to deal with my case. Each visit necessitated
a long taking-down of particulars before the man behind the desk
could reach the decision that such matters did not fall within his
jurisdiction. My main anxiety was that we might not find anybody
to deal with the case until after the holiday, which lasted another
three days. I would gladly have surrendered the gun and paid a
large fine on the spot.

At last, our fifth port of call, we came to a palatial building set
back in a garden. Smart sentries stood at the gate and I noticed
they were military rather than gendarmerie. Our delegation was
led into an office where several elegant army officers discussed the
problem with us in French. Then the Consul and I were ushered
into another room, and introduced to the occupant, a general.

We sat down and chatted pleasantly about the weather and
the necessity of carrying guns in Afghanistan. Finally a bell was
pressed and an orderly hurried in bearing bottles of Coca-Cola
and a printed form. The charming general signed the form and
handed it to me together with the controversial Luger.

'Now you will be all right for a fortnight,' he said kindly. His signature indicated that he was head of the Security Forces of Iran. As such he was presumably responsible for seeing that there was no repetition of the Iraq affair in his country. He evidently believed that I was not the assassin type.

21

ASTARA

WHENEVER I wanted something from an official source, it somehow turned out to be a public holiday. Owing to the *Moharram* celebrations, it was impossible to get a permit to cover the next stage of the journey—along the Caspian as far as the frontier town of Astara and thence across to Tabriz. I had heard of an Englishman being recently turned back from Astara, but rather than spend any more hot and expensive time in Teheran I determined to go ahead and hope for the best.

We crossed the Elburz by the now familiar Chalus route. The incipient Motel we had noted beside the Caspian on our earlier trip was now in full swing. The car park was filled with smart American-made cars and the beach was gay with coloured umbrellas. The 'Ghoo Trio' was playing at the end of a rickety wooden pier where two or three couples were jigging up and down to a foxtrot. Coca-Cola, obeying the dictates of supply and demand, had shot up to twenty rials a bottle and not even iced at that.

The moment of decision faced us at Rasht. Should we continue by the normal route through Pahlevi where, from our previous visit we knew there was a checkpoint, or should we take the road, marked with a dotted line on the map, that ran due west to rejoin the coast road some thirty miles further on? The second alternative would have been an obvious choice had I not heard that the inland route was never used. However, as I wanted to see the jungle country of Gilan I decided to put my trust in Land-Rovers and attempt it.

It was perfectly easy at first. But beyond the first village a policeman barred the way. Taking care not to mention Astara I named the next village as my destination, about fifteen miles away. But he was not stopping me, it appeared, to question my right to be there, but to point out that the road I was planning to take was impassable. I was asking for exact information about the nature and extent of this 'impassability' when a crowd began to collect around the car. A young man with a bicycle appeared on the scene and entered into an earnest discussion with the policeman. He seemed to hold the opinion that the road *was* passable, and was prepared to prove his point by coming with us. But everyone else agreed with the policeman and there were many knowing headshakes as we drove off to put the question to the test.

The first hazard, soon reached, was a river. It was wide but it had a firm-looking bottom and though a little apprehensive as a result of previous experiences, I drove boldly over and gained the other bank without difficulty to the cheers of the trailing on-lookers. I began to think all would now be easy.

The man on the bicycle, who seemed to take the whole matter with the greatest seriousness, as if his reputation depended on the outcome, led us down a sandy track that ran deep into the Caspian lowlands. It was hot and damp; tasselled corn grew twice as high as a man; the blackening sunflowers, often six to a stalk, could barely hold up their enormous heads; cow parsley grew like parasols; tobacco flowers were turning to seed; the heavy air hummed with insects. Fructidor was in with a vengeance.

We were not able to give our attention to the fascinating landscape for long. The second hazard was soon upon us—a narrow bridge made of turfed-over logs crossing a muddy stream about fifteen feet wide. There was no more than a five-foot drop on either side, but had we gone over the edge we should never have got out again. I once toppled a car into a canal in the Camargue and it was an experience I did not wish to repeat.

The man on the bicycle seemed to think we could take it in our stride and waved us on confidently from the far side. But when I measured the width of the bridge and compared it with the car I found that there were no more than three inches in favour of the bridge. Added to which the edges were crumbling and the logs were rotten. I very nearly decided against it, but Diana urged me on, thus considerately offering herself as a scape-goat should things go wrong. By propping up the weak spots with petrol cans and sticks and driving with precise accuracy along the only possible line, I managed to get the car across. But I was dripping with sweat and shaking with a nervous tremor.

I had not been long congratulating myself on my skill and daring when we came to another similar bridge. But this one looked entirely impossible, sections of it were actually an inch narrower than the car, the logs were even more rotten and part of the middle had caved in.

I considered the problem for some minutes, anxiously pacing up and down, measuring, prodding and propping. A crowd of villagers had appeared from the fields and were watching every move. I felt utterly defeated until an old man led me to a pile of poplar logs behind the hedge. Willing hands helped to carry these to the bridge and they were laid in position at certain strategic intervals. The only hope was to drive across sufficiently fast for the rotten parts to hold and sufficiently under control to keep the wheels from slipping off the logs. We got across. I do not know how.

By now I had had enough, and I earnestly questioned the escorting bicyclist, who I was certain was plotting to lead me on to my doom, as to exactly what lay ahead. I think he measured passability in terms of his bicycle for he cried, 'Hup! Hup! OK! OK!' and then there were four more bridges, each one of which reduced me to a quivering jelly.

Then came the worst of the lot. It was as narrow as the first and completely rotten, with the added hazard that the ditch was twice as deep. Praying to St Christopher I took it straight and fast. As we gained the far side the wheels got caught in a branch and the bridge slowly collapsed. But by some miracle the front wheels held their grip and in a cloud of dirt and debris the car clawed itself to safety.

The above summary of the battle of the bridges is restrained. It had taken six terrible hours to travel as many miles.

'Finish bridges,' our guide assured us, and we were having a short self-congratulatory interlude when we saw a uniformed figure wheeling a bicycle towards us down the forest track ahead. He looked us over with a suspicious and intolerant eye, then fiercely waved us back in the direction whence we had come. 'Hup! Hup!' I cried, pointing in the direction we were heading. And to show that I meant what I said I drove on into the gloomy wood. I had gone about twenty yards when I came to a sorry stop, wheels spinning and the axles deep in jungle mud.

The soldier (I was relieved to find he was not a gendarme with constitutional powers to give us orders) again made signs that we should go back. I got out of the car and walked with him to the bridge, pointing out that it had broken and that there was no possibility of crossing it again. But you cannot go on! he seemed to be trying to say . . . Enormous trees lay across the track through the forest! He had to walk round them with his bicycle! And then there were more rivers! Two rivers! With steep banks and no bridges at all! . . . This was too much: if what the soldier said was true we were stuck in the middle of the Caspian jungle, miles from anywhere, with no food and no hope of getting out. The idiotic bicyclist who had got us into this ridiculous position could go back to his village and they could all have a good laugh at his and our expense.

How far on were the trees across the track? Ten minutes on the bicycle, said the soldier. Darkness was falling fast; I grabbed his bicycle and peddled off down the gloomy path to reconnoitre, leaving him to protect Diana from the dangers of the surrounding forest.

It was not easy to ride through the mud. The two-barred British-made bicycle was appallingly uncomfortable and before long the chain came off. Imagining all sorts of growlings in the forest I used it as a scooter and scooted as fast as I could through the shadows. It seemed an age before I came to a long stretch of track across which small saplings, recently felled, lay in tangled masses. These were certainly not the forest giants of the soldier's description and it seemed that with determination and an axe a path might well be cleared. There was no question of investigating the rivers. First obstacles first!

I returned to the car to find Diana still intact but worried by my long absence and by the stories the soldier had been telling her about tigers and robbers. She was in no danger from him apparently, for he had explained, with a simple drawing, that he only liked big women. Russian women all had big breasts, he said. Wonderful!

The soldier—he was a sergeant—seemed to think it would be unsafe for us to spend the night in the forest among the bandits (a knife passed across his throat), and the tigers (a sinister growl). He recommended that we take our valuables from the car and come with him to look for shelter.

We must have walked for an hour down the muddy path, noisy with the croak of frogs in the lagoons and ditches and mosquitoes buzzing about our ears. I had heard that malaria had been wiped out along the Caspian, but the sergeant thought differently and kept saying, 'Malaria! Malaria!' in a very discouraging way. Then unaccountably, he grew merry and started singing songs.

At last little lights began to illuminate straw-thatched huts and the outlines of their owners could be seen squatting on their verandas. Our soldier went hopefully towards the first house, but they would not take us in because there were women, and most of these houses had only one room. At last we met a lonely old man walking down the road, who offered us his roof. We climbed over a stile and down an overgrown garden to his little crazy cottage. Then he lit a hurricane lamp and bade us sit on the veranda while he went to fetch some food, returning with a melon and some bread. The old man, with grizzled hair, a roman nose and hollow cheeks that suggested the ravages of malaria, was obviously extremely poor. But he had great natural dignity and looked after us with patrician charm.

With moths fluttering round the lamp and giant spiders crawling on the wall, we sat and talked long into the night, and though I knew no Persian I seemed to know exactly what was said, especially by the sergeant who had great powers of mime. He told of his experiences fighting the Russians—in these very woods —along that track their tanks had rolled—he, the soldier, had accounted for one, two, three, four Russians with his rifle. Shells had fallen . . . boom, boom . . . but he had been unhurt. Look, a medal!

I could not quite make out what action against the Russians he could have referred to, unless he was engaged in guerrilla action before the Russians withdrew from the Caspian provinces after the war. He was hardly old enough to have taken part in the operations against Kuchik Khan, when British armoured cars led by Major-General 'Stalky' Dunsterville were in the offing, nor to have assisted Riza Khan in overthrowing the Soviet Republic of Gilan.

Our host suddenly decided that the car and its contents would be unsafe where I had left it, and though I tried to prevent him he insisted on going to guard it, producing an ancient flintlock rifle with an immensely long barrel from the recesses of his hut. Armed also with his hatchet, he set off into the night.

Human nature is droll. For some reason, perhaps because he

had decided we were friends, the sergeant rather shiftily came out with the information that if the truth was known our woodcutter host could probably deal with the trees on the track and that the rivers he had described as impassable, in fact could be crossed lower down. Having got this off his chest he went to sleep. His initial discouragement must have been purely psychological.

Very early in the morning the soldier crept over to me and whispered that he had to be on his way. Would I help him over the stile with his bicycle? Diana lay sleeping fitfully on the wooden floor; I drove away the mosquitoes that hovered round her face. A monotonous hum seemed to come from the surrounding forest as I walked with the soldier down the little garden path.

At the stile he kept pointing admiringly at my watch and then disparagingly at his own, which apparently did not keep good time. I gathered that he wanted mine so that he would not be late for parade (he urgently saluted an imaginary superior). I pretended not to understand for as long as I could, but he went on and on about it, insisting that he would be returning later and would give it back at the car. On this understanding I handed over my really quite valuable watch. It was the last I saw of it. Some villagers who knew him said that he was on his way to Rasht and would not be returning for weeks.

There was no chance of going to sleep again. It was not yet dawn when Diana and I set off to walk to the car. When we came up to it there was the old man, sitting cross-legged on the bonnet with the rifle over his knee. He must have had a miserable night, thinking, perhaps, that to get inside would be a breach of good manners.

After a cup of tea we felt better able to consider the problem of our onward progress. The first necessity was to cross the morass that lay immediately ahead (we were deep in the province of Gilan, and *gil* is a word meaning mud). The old man's axe was an invaluable ally and by slashing down branches and laying them across the track we made a tolerable causeway.

Then came the belt of cut-down trees. This extended for about a hundred yards and though each was no larger than a man's wrist it was clear that some hard work lay ahead of us. The old man set to work with his axe and was soon joined by other axe-men who came down the path on their way to work. In this part

of the world the hatchet was almost obligatory wear (in neigh-
bouring Tabaristan, which means 'the country of the hatchets',
the inhabitants are said to use their hatchets to kill tigers, which
they follow up on foot).

After three hours work we had cleared a path which we crashed
through in as many minutes. I rewarded the old man with 500 rials
(about £3 10s) for his goodness, a princely sum for him; finding
himself so rich he offered to come on with us to the next village,
where he would be able to buy tobacco. His axe was still at our
disposal, he indicated, shaking it in the air and running a finger
along its trusty edge.

It was well for us that he came. There was more bog ahead,
more fallen trees, and streams crossing the path like varicose
veins. Our final labour, with the rice-thatched village in sight
beyond, was to cross an open ditch full of black mud. We cut
down branches and laid them across the bottom, but I drove over
too fast and the twigs got tangled up in the wheels. Twenty
stalwart villagers came to the rescue and dug us out with spades
and soon we were washing off the mud in which we, they and
the car were completely covered, in a clear stream that ran through
the village square.

Ours was the first car ever to come that way, said the villagers,
shaking their heads and plying us with tea. But a few miles on we
should reach a good road and then we should have no more
trouble.

It was as they said, for once: we soon came upon the main
Rasht–Astara road.

We reached Astara at about 4 p.m. and had barely passed the
old Russian Fisheries building on the sandy coastal strip outside
the town, when we came up against the checkpoint, manned by
soldiers with tommy guns in US-type steel helmets. A soldier
hopped aboard and directed us to a nearby military barracks.

We waited with some anxiety while our papers were being
inspected. There was a distinct possibility that we might have to
return to Rasht, which would have meant a detour of hundreds of
miles to reach Tabriz. But they must have thought that as we had
got so far and been cleared by the control at Pahlavi we were all
right, for our passports were returned and we were set on the road
to Tabriz.

We came up against Russia almost immediately. A river ran parallel to the road on its way to the Caspian. On the far bank was a line of barbed wire and beyond, less than two hundred yards from us, was the regulation wooden watchtower from which the Red Flag flew and Russian soldiers looked out over Iranian territory.

Road and frontier followed the river up a leafy gorge on the far slope of which a sinuous scar wound through the trees, the ploughed strip across which no man might pass undetected. Another Russian watchtower now appeared and I stopped the car to take a discreet photograph. I had just clicked the shutter when a black Plymouth came noiselessly up from behind and stopped behind us. I barely had time to push the camera into a bag before a soldier ran towards me shouting and pointing at the binoculars that I had forgotten were still hanging round my neck. He did not appear to have seen the camera and the crime under review was presumably that of studying the Soviet Union through binoculars. The excitable soldier was now joined by an officer, who dealt with the matter more calmly, and politely asked to see our papers. Why had I stopped the car? he asked. I explained quite frankly that I wanted to have a closer look at Russia—if that was a crime it was surely a crime against the Russians, not against Iran. This argument was effective, for having done no more than point at my binoculars and shake his head roguishly, the officer, together with the soldier, got back into their car and waved me on ahead. They stayed behind us for some way but we only had three active cylinders and went so slowly that they eventually got bored and roared on past us.

The river now tumbled noisily down the gorge, the country was rugged with tangled woodland on our side and more ordered conifers on the other. For twenty miles or so the scar snaked opposite, with occasional watchtowers on the Russian side and patrols of soldiers and green, red and white markers on ours. Then the scar jagged off round a spur and our road began to curve towards the south. Our flirtation with the frontier was over.

The country opened up, but the hills remained, the western extension of the Elburz, with Kum-i-Savalan, 14,000 feet, lying ahead. The sun was setting behind fields of sunflowers and the chilly air was suffused with an unusual lambency, stimulating and at the same time sad. Passing several military posts we wound down on to an upland plain, lately shorn of wheat, and parked for the night in the middle of a windy field.

Next morning was cold and damp and drizzly. The engine would not start despite the reluctant shovings of a lorry. The Army saved the day, and we held up a whole convoy while their leader did something with a cigarette lighter to the coils.

Delayed by engine trouble and tyre bursts we did not reach Tabriz until the evening. Haggard and dirty and shivering with cold we booked in at the Metropole. After a hot shower there was dinner in the familiar dining-room, sadly without the accompaniment of the Armenian trio, for it was still *Moharram* and no time for manifestations of gaiety.

22

JULFA

SINCE MARCH, when the Shah had opened the railway line from Teheran to Tabriz, American diesels had been running regularly along British rails lying on French sleepers. The line continued beyond Tabriz to Julfa, on the frontier of Soviet Nakhichevan, where it linked up with the Russian railway system. Until recently this stretch of line, originally laid by the Russians, had been their wide five-foot gauge, but it had now been converted to the standard Iranian gauge. Recent agreements permitted the passage of tourists via that frontier, and I had heard it said that the cheapest way to travel from Teheran to Europe was via Moscow. Under the same agreement the Iranians were allowed to fly passengers between Tabriz and Baku, but difficulties were being raised by the Russians owing to the fact that Iranair employed a number of American pilots.

A visit to Julfa, I thought, would be worth the hundred-mile detour north of the road to Turkey. But it was not the best moment to ask for permission to go there: following the events in Iraq Russian troops were manœuvring in Armenia and Soviet Azerbidjan and the Persian side would be fully alerted.

I was not altogether surprised when the young deputy governor, who had promised to help me on my first visit to the town, pointed out these very objections. He referred the question to the other personages having audience in his office at the time, who happened to be the Commander of the Army in Tabriz and the Chief of Police respectively. They shook their heads in a depressingly discouraging way.

'Am I to take this as a categorical refusal?' I asked. Persians do not like the categorical: the deputy governor qualified himself by saying:

'It is not for me to order yes or no. You can now go and ask the Governor-General, if you wish.'

I sent in my card to M. Zand, the Governor-General, and waited my turn in the well-furnished ante-room to his office. Important government officials are very approachable in Iran,

The wrong road to Astara, M.A. in ditch

Russian lookout tower, frontier beyond Astara

even to the most humble, and I was soon shown into the presence. M. Zand, a short dapper man in a dark suit, greeted me kindly. He asked me why on earth I wished to go to such a terrible place as Julfa. I could only say that I wished to write about it and that writers could find something to say about even the most unlikely places. M. Zand reminded me of the military anxiety on that frontier and told me that he had recently refused permission to two Germans who wished to go that way.

Then for some reason the Governor-General decided to make an exception. He wrote out a permit which was to be stamped by the police and the military. His signature would ensure that theirs was forthcoming.

'Ce n'est pas un joli endroit, Julfa! Nous sommes en train de le reconstruire,' he said, as I left. It was as if he was apologizing in advance for whatever deficiencies I might find in the place.

Having obtained the appropriate counter-signatures we left Tabriz in the afternoon. At Marand we took the road to the north and followed the railway line over a bare, sandy plain. Lorries carrying steel girders and heavy crates from the direction of Russia seemed to be doing the railway's job, for we never saw a train pass along that line.

By nightfall we had reached a low line of hills about fifteen miles from the frontier. I parked the car in a sandy depression fifty yards from the road and there we went to sleep. I was awakened some hours later by the sound of an approaching vehicle and bright headlights illuminated my bedroom in the back of the car. Peering out, I saw three soldiers descending from a jeep. They must have been surprised to see a para-military vehicle, with no recognizable markings, right in the middle of their manœuvre area. But they were reassured by my documents and by the fact that I could point to a flat tyre, just observed by me, to justify our particular stopping-place. They gave us an apple apiece and withdrew into the darkness.

In the morning we passed other signs of military activity. Small groups of tanks were lurking in hollow ground, jeeps and trucks were stirring up clouds of dust on the hillside. A check-point, manned by a young officer, passed us through and we came on to flat ground at the far extremity of which could be seen the tall water-tower of Julfa. I was uncertain whether first to present my credentials to the authorities and run the risk of circumscription, or to see what I could see before being challenged. As no 'authorities' were apparent I began a small private tour of inspection.

Julfa was no more than a conglomeration of railway sidings and wired-in dumps with a mean street of stone buildings and seedy shops and stalls. A few houses were being built on the outskirts, which may have been the 'reconstruction' referred to by M. Zand. Behind the town the river Aras ran, the classical Araxes, backed on the Russian side by stony hills. The river, crossed by a shining steel railway bridge, marked the frontier. (The Russians had put up plans for an irrigation project on the Aras, which was to bring great benefits to both sides. It would also have meant the presence of the Russians across their frontier and the Persians had not yet accepted the proposals. A similar plan for the Oxus has for a long time been under discussion with the Afghans.) On the far side were a number of houses and what looked like a large factory, but was in fact a locomotive repair shop. Nearby, on the flanking hill, was the inevitable wooden watchtower.

Parking the car behind the water-tower we followed the railway line on foot into a big wired-in enclosure where goods were in the process of being unloaded. The flat trucks carried enormous wooden packing-cases many of which were stamped tantalizingly in Russian script. The east European countries were well represented, especially Czechoslovakia, who had consigned large quantities of galoshes. It might be thought that the Persians were preparing for a wet winter: but like the Turks they wear this most unsuitable footgear rain or shine, protecting not their shoes but their bare feet.

Other items that lay around included brightly painted tractors from Poland, shiny dynamos from East Germany, and Russian motor-cars. Also from Russia were the huge piles of wooden railway sleepers: their intermediate destination was an American-built plant where they would be processed with pentichlorofinol, said to be an improvement on the conventional creosote.

As we came out of the gate at the other end of the enclosure we were challenged by a soldier. I handed him my permit and he disappeared with it into a stone building, emerging shortly with a fiery major and two other soldiers. The major's appearance belied his manner. He was not at all fierce and most politely asked if there was anything he could do for us. I asked if I could take a look round, and instead of saying anything so churlish as 'you seem to have taken a look round already', he took us on a conducted tour.

The highpoint of the tour was the passenger train in the main station, which we had not reached on our private inspection. A great black engine with its name on the side in Russian script and a large hammer and sickle over the front end waited to haul the train over the bridge and into Russia. Several passenger coaches were attached. That day there were no happy tourists peering from the windows, but behind the green curtains of the Pullman car, which had its name on the side (perhaps a Russian version of 'Ermyntrude' or 'Dorothy' such as may be found on their British equivalent), one forlorn passenger was visible, sitting at a table and patiently reading by the light of a frilly orange lamp. I asked the major if I could photograph the train but he said it was forbidden.

Our guide, who was in fact the Military Commandant of Julfa, invited us into his house. We passed through a flowery courtyard and were introduced to his wife, a plump and smiling lady who plied us with grapes, biscuits and sugar sweets. I asked her if she did not sometimes get a little bored being stuck in Julfa, and she replied that except for the heat she was very happy, and Tabriz was not too far away. I asked the commandant if he ever met his Russian opposites and to my surprise he said that he had only done so once, when he accompanied a mission to discuss an American aeroplane that had crashed over the frontier.

We did not accept their kind invitation to stay for lunch. It was still early and there was a chance of reaching Turkey that night.

Leaving Julfa we naturally took the road direct to Khoi, the third side of the triangle. But after some miles we were stopped at a military control point and a young officer pointed out that my permit only authorized us to travel by the way we had come. It would have been a great inconvenience to return via Marand and I was relieved when the officer accepted the authority of the Military Commander at Julfa, who I claimed had directed us that way. As we had already passed through the main military concentration, which had included cruiser tanks and light field guns, he must have appreciated that no purpose would be served by sending us back. A soldier was instructed to accompany us, more I think because he wanted a lift than to act as an escort, and we carried him to Khoi without further incident or interest.

While waiting for the Khoi police to provide the necessary papers for us to leave Persia (an exit permit as well as an entry visa was obligatory), we lunched in a simple restaurant on thin Iranian stew. Outside a bus was preparing to leave for Reziyah, near the great lake of Urmiah about fifty miles to the south. A friendly schoolmaster, with whom I had been discussing Reziyah's most famous son, Zoroaster, said: 'Why not come too? It is not a bad place.' If I had been more confident about the car I should have offered him a lift, for as well as Reziyah I was anxious to see what progress was being made in the construction of the defensive line guarding the approach up the valley of the Rowanduz to the great oil regions of Iraq. The American Army was said to be superintending its construction, and I wondered what had been the effect of the Iraqui revolution on their plans.

Events in Iraq seemed to have affected the Turkish frontier zone, for we were stopped by soldiers at a village about ten miles short of Turkey, and for over an hour sat by the roadside waiting to be passed through. I fretted at the delay and finally stalked into the hotel, part of which had been taken over by the military. In an inner room I found a group of Iranian officers joking and laughing with a German couple whose particulars they were facetiously investigating and laboriously inscribing on a form. I did not wish to break up a jolly party but as I wanted to cross the frontier that day I asked them to give me immediate attention. They seemed a little upset at my interruption, but finally, after a string of questions, a stamp was affixed on a piece of paper, which apparently had to be countersigned by a captain. Where was the captain? Oh, somewhere in the town! Impatient now I went off in search of their superior and finally found him shopping in the bazaar. The Iranian Army seemed to be making a regular field day of it, for just then a party of officers on horses rode by accompanied by a pretty girl with streaming blonde hair. Shortly afterwards a jeep roared by with more soldiers and a ravishing dark girl at the wheel. We wondered who on earth they could be.

There was now little time to gain the frontier before it packed up for the night. After ten minutes driving I decided it would be better to stay the night in the town and cross the following morning. I was influenced in this decision by a desire to solve the mystery of the two girls, and by a feeling that something lucky would turn up.

In the dining-room of the small hotel we found the German couple, now augmented by several other German couples, but there was no sign of the girls. The Germans made me feel a little guilty by telling me that after I had left the room where they were being interviewed, one of the officers had said pathetically: 'Do you think he was really angry with us? You see our life is so dull that it is nice for us to talk to travellers.' Confirming my hunch that something lucky would turn up they offered me £10 in Turkish money against payment in England at some future date. This was most welcome as I had insufficient money even to get as far as Ankara.

The mystery girls materialized the following morning. We had just passed through the Iranian frontier when they arrived in a French car. We were waiting to be passed through by the Turks, when our old enemy the plump policeman (now splendid in his white summer uniform) suddenly halted his course towards us and returned to his office. I thought he was planning his revenge and after a short impatient wait I hurried after him. To my surprise I saw the two girls in the process of having their papers cleared. They had apparently come through a passage from the Persian side and had been given immediate attention at our expense. I sat down beside them looking vexed and made a mild protest to the blonde girl, who spoke excellent English. 'We were passed through specially because Monique's father is Prime Minister of Iran.' The blonde was Finnish and had been at school with Monique (whose name was Icqbal) in Germany, and had lately been staying with her in Teheran. I conceded them their place in the queue on the grounds of charm rather than connections. Finally it was our turn. The plump policeman seemed pleased enough to see us again and we forgave him his former tiresomeness. And so we passed through into Turkey.

I was now in a hurry to get back to England; we had been away for over three months and had travelled over 15,000 miles. I had seen enough of the 'Underbelly of the Bear' and any ideas I may have had about attempting the Kars route in reverse were abandoned. Instead we decided to take the central road through

Ercinjan. At Doubayazid, of evil memory, we bought twelve tins of *dolmas* (vine leaves stuffed with rice and pine kernels) and were heartily sick of them by the time we reached Istanbul five days later.

Brewster was still in residence at the Hilton, though much to his annoyance he had been forced to share a room with another airman. When he saw us he said: 'Hey! Where have you been all this time? You look like a couple of *shishkebabs*!' This reference to the Turkish national dish, meat grilled on a skewer, alluded to our lean and sun-baked exteriors. But a week of working through the list of 'delectable Turkish, American and International dishes' and lying around the swimming pool with Ergun and others put us in better shape. The only thing that failed to recover was the car, owing to its being driven from Greece with a holed radiator and a broken fan. It was a total wreck by the time it reached Dover, where it was ignominiously pushed off the boat and sold to a scrap dealer for £50.